The Cast of the Kingdom

Biblical characters who model faith

The staff and students of

Ridley Hall CAMBRIDGE

CANTERBURY
PRESS
Norwich

© Ridley Hall 2008

First published in 2008 by the Canterbury Press Norwich
(a publishing imprint of Hymns Ancient & Modern Limited,
a registered charity)
13–17 Long Lane, London EC1A 9PN

www.scm-canterburypress.co.uk

Except where indicated, scripture quotations are taken
from the Holy Bible, Today's New International Version®
TNIV®. Copyright © 2001, 2005 by International Bible
Society. Used by permission of IBS-STL U.S.
All rights reserved worldwide.

British Library Cataloguing in Publication data

A catalogue record for this book is available
from the British Library

ISBN 978-1-85311-933-0

Typeset by Regent Typesetting, London
Printed in Great Britain by
CPI Bookmarque, Croydon, CR0 4TD

Contents

During the weeks that we were working on this book it was announced that our former Principal, Christopher Cocksworth, had been selected to become the Bishop of Coventry. Therefore we dedicate this book to Bishop Chris, in gratitude for the wonderful years that he spent at the helm of Ridley Hall.

Using this Book

In a group

Ridley Hall's Lent meditations have proved to be excellent 'starters' for small group discussion. The experience of many groups has been that simply talking about how the prior week's reflections have spoken to group members has been enough to generate conversations and prompt insights that have been highly valued. These have, in turn, built confidence and mutuality, sometimes to an unexpected degree. Perhaps this is because the meditations derive from the wide-ranging life experiences of Ridley's students, and so easily provoke empathy and establish common ground with the readers.

As an individual

- Each day during Lent, set aside some time in a quiet place. You will need only this book, as the relevant Bible passages accompany each reflection.
- Do whatever helps you to relax – sit somewhere quiet, make a drink, take some deep breaths.
- Pray for God's Spirit to guide you before you read.
- Read the Bible passage set for the day – slowly – and think about what it might be saying.
- Then read the reflection for the day – again slowly – and pause for thought as you go. How does it relate to the Bible passage? Is there anything in the reflection which is similar to or different from anything you have experienced or thought before?

- When you have read and reflected, pray about what you have read and ask God what he might be saying to you through it; you might like to use the Lord's Prayer to finish.

The Daily Reflections

Joshua 14.6–13

Now the people of Judah approached Joshua at Gilgal, and Caleb son of Jephunneh the Kenizzite said to him, 'You know what the LORD said to Moses the man of God at Kadesh Barnea about you and me. I was forty years old when Moses the servant of the LORD sent me from Kadesh Barnea to explore the land. And I brought him back a report according to my convictions, but the others who went up with me made the hearts of the people melt in fear. I, however, followed the LORD my God wholeheartedly. So on that day Moses swore to me, "The land on which your feet have walked will be your inheritance and that of your children forever, because you have followed the LORD my God wholeheartedly."

'Now then, just as the LORD promised, he has kept me alive for forty-five years since the time he said this to Moses, while Israel moved about in the wilderness. So here I am today, eighty-five years old! I am still as strong today as the day Moses sent me out; I'm just as vigorous to go out to battle now as I was then. Now give me this hill country that the LORD promised me that day. You yourself heard then that the Anakites were there and their cities were large and fortified, but, the LORD helping me, I will drive them out just as he said.'

Then Joshua blessed Caleb son of Jephunneh and gave him Hebron as his inheritance. So Hebron has belonged to Caleb son of Jephunneh the Kenizzite ever since, because he followed the LORD, the God of Israel, wholeheartedly.

Caleb: Wholeheartedness

We might get a bit uncomfortable these days reading of spies and invasions, but we can still learn a lot from Caleb. My goodness, I hope that when I'm eighty-five years old I'm still as enthusiastic about my faith and as committed to seeing God's purposes fulfilled as this man. When most of us would be thinking about taking life a little more easily, Caleb is still raring to go. He is described as someone who followed God wholeheartedly; we can see that in action at the beginning of his story in Numbers 13 and 14.

Caleb was wholehearted, not half-hearted. He didn't just follow God when things were going well, or when it suited him and wouldn't cost him anything, only to give up the moment things got difficult. Rather, Caleb really stepped up to the mark when the going got tough.

You know the kind of person who only ever sees all the problems and potential pitfalls involved in doing something, who only ever sees the reasons for not doing it? The sort of person who writes something off as a failure before it's even started? That's not Caleb! Caleb wasn't easily deterred. Instead, he sought to instil confidence in others: 'If this is what God wants, we can do it.' This was not blind optimism. Caleb simply took God at his word.

Caleb's heart was undivided. He wasn't torn between serving God's purposes and looking after his own interests. He was wholeheartedly God's. God had all of him.

Lord God, give me Caleb's wholeheartedness to see your purposes worked out in the place to which you've called me. Amen.

John 4.28–29, 39–42

Then, leaving her water jar, the woman went back to the town and said to the people, 'Come, see a man who told me everything I ever did. Could this be the Messiah?'

Many of the Samaritans from that town believed in him because of the woman's testimony, 'He told me everything I ever did.' So when the Samaritans came to him, they urged him to stay with them, and he stayed two days. And because of his words many more became believers.

They said to the woman, 'We no longer believe just because of what you said; now we have heard for ourselves, and we know that this man really is the Saviour of the world.'

The Woman at the Well: Honest Evangelism

Things had not gone well. Five husbands already. And now number six, who wasn't even her husband. Whatever her motivations, I can't imagine that life had gone according to plan for the woman at the well. Now here she is, shunned by society; a social outcast.

But then she meets Jesus and begins to wonder, is he the Messiah? When she discovers that he knows the skeletons hiding in her cupboard, she doesn't run from him or try to deny her past. Instead, with boldness, urgency and honesty, she tells the people about her encounter with her question, 'Could this be the Messiah?'

This woman had guts. She went to those who had looked down upon her. She must have known that her own testimony would be questioned. Conscious that people in town knew about her dubious past, she suddenly had the spirit to face those who might want to stone her, and tell what had happened. Because of her, the people of the town were moved to come out and meet Christ for themselves.

Sometimes we have to go into situations where we are uncomfortable, where we would usually feel small, inferior and, well, useless and terrified! We may also think we have to know a great deal and have great confidence to be a good witness. This woman shows us that the real hope that Christ brings is so great that it's not impossible to share our own experiences of Jesus, even in our questions.

Gracious God, fill us with boldness to tell others of your love and mercy with honesty. In Jesus' name, Amen.

John 1.19–31

Now this was John's testimony when the Jewish leaders in Jerusalem sent priests and Levites to ask him who he was. He did not fail to confess, but confessed freely, 'I am not the Messiah.'

They asked him, 'Then who are you? Are you Elijah?'

He said, 'I am not.'

'Are you the Prophet?'

He answered, 'No.'

Finally they said, 'Who are you? Give us an answer to take back to those who sent us. What do you say about yourself?'

John replied in the words of Isaiah the prophet, 'I am the voice of one calling in the wilderness, "Make straight the way for the Lord."'

Now the Pharisees who had been sent questioned him, 'Why then do you baptize if you are not the Messiah, nor Elijah, nor the Prophet?'

'I baptize with water,' John replied, 'but among you stands one you do not know. He is the one who comes after me, the thongs of whose sandals I am not worthy to untie.'

This all happened at Bethany on the other side of the Jordan, where John was baptizing.

The next day John saw Jesus coming toward him and said, 'Look, the Lamb of God, who takes away the sin of the world! This is the one I meant when I said, "A man who comes after me has surpassed me because he was before me." I myself did not know him, but the reason I came baptizing with water was that he might be revealed to Israel.'

John the Baptist: Humility

He receives the ball on the halfway line and feels inspired to push forward. This is the moment, his moment. He looks up and blazes in, cutting a neat line through the midfield. His feet dance and the ball moves ever closer to the goal. The crowd are a mass of open mouths, willing him on. They need this win and he feels that pressure inside him like iron. This is where it gets dangerous for most people. A speculative strike from here could see the ball in the net and win the game. But not him, he knows he can't go all the way and he's happy with that. He's seen others before take that step too far, ending their moment of glory by giving the ball away and having to chase it back from the other team. This isn't about him, it never has been. In fact, he's just glad to be on the pitch. As the last defender closes him down he knows what to do. He waits, and then releases the ball to his captain. The path to goal now lies open and the attack moves on. Along with the spectators, he watches his captain apply the finishing touch. Joy rises up inside. His part is over.

Humility: a word turned into a life by John the Baptist. 'He must increase, but I must decrease' (John 3.30). We all have our part to play for God, and only we can play it. But our part is never the whole story.

Father, thank you for having laid out a path for each one of us. Help me to walk along it with humility. Amen.

Judges 4.4–10

Now Deborah, a prophet, the wife of Lappidoth, was leading Israel at that time. She held court under the Palm of Deborah between Ramah and Bethel in the hill country of Ephraim, and the Israelites went up to her to have their disputes decided. She sent for Barak son of Abinoam from Kedesh in Naphtali and said to him, 'The LORD, the God of Israel, commands you: "Go, take with you ten thousand men of Naphtali and Zebulun and lead them up to Mount Tabor. I will lead Sisera, the commander of Jabin's army, with his chariots and his troops to the Kishon River and give him into your hands."'

Barak said to her, 'If you go with me, I will go; but if you don't go with me, I won't go.'

'Certainly I will go with you,' said Deborah. 'But because of the course you are taking, the honour will not be yours, for the LORD will deliver Sisera into the hands of a woman.' So Deborah went with Barak to Kedesh. There Barak summoned Zebulun and Naphtali, and ten thousand men went up under his command. Deborah also went up with him.

Deborah: Confident Yet Flexible

I love the surprises that come in scripture, for they give me confidence that God can act surprisingly even in my own life. And there are few more surprising, topsy-turvy passages than this one, which speaks of a woman of fiery courage and faith. There she is, Deborah, a woman in a society where the leaders are all men, a wife in a culture where she is supposed to play a passive role. But does that stop Deborah? Not at all! She already has a track record of prophesying and ruling Israel, and now she's about to see off Israel's great enemy, the Philistines. What has enabled her to break through tradition and exceed expectations? She has confidence in the Lord, whom she knows intimately. He is central in what she says and who she is.

I'm much more like Barak, a steady worker, frightened to death about putting his faith to the test. Yet it's Barak that Deborah needs, just as much as Barak needs Deborah. Deborah is not a fighter. Perhaps (I like to think) she regards battles as a rather boring and messy business. But if the Lord is behind the plan, nothing else really matters, and Deborah is willing to go.

I admire men and women like Deborah, who know the Lord so deeply that nothing is impossible. I thank God for their confidence. But I also thank God that an inspired Deborah is flexible enough to accompany an uncertain Barak. Together they gain a great victory.

Lord, please help me to live and speak with the confidence and flexibility of Deborah. Amen.

Acts 4.34–37 (NIV)

There were no needy persons among them. For from time to time those who owned land or houses sold them, brought the money from the sales and put it at the apostles' feet, and it was distributed to anyone who had need.

Joseph, a Levite from Cyprus, whom the apostles called Barnabas (which means 'son of encouragement'), sold a field he owned and brought the money and put it at the apostles' feet.

Acts 9.26–28

When Saul came to Jerusalem, he tried to join the disciples, but they were all afraid of him, not believing that he really was a disciple. But Barnabas took him and brought him to the apostles. He told them how Saul on his journey had seen the Lord and that the Lord had spoken to him, and how in Damascus he had preached fearlessly in the name of Jesus. So Saul stayed with them and moved about freely in Jerusalem, speaking boldly in the name of the Lord.

Acts 15.36–39

Some time later Paul said to Barnabas, 'Let us go back and visit the believers in all the towns where we preached the word of the Lord and see how they are doing.' Barnabas wanted to take John, also called Mark, with them, but Paul did not think it wise to take him, because he had deserted them in Pamphylia and had not continued with them in the work. They had such a sharp disagreement that they parted company. Barnabas took Mark and sailed for Cyprus.

Barnabas: Generous Encouragement

I owe a great deal in my life to those who have given me generous encouragement. When I was leading a small church on a council estate, I went to the minister of a large town-centre church and said, 'We are going to shut up shop on Sunday evenings and join you. It will encourage our twenty folk by joining in with your six hundred.' 'No, don't,' he said, 'I will encourage our members who live near you to join you.' He did, and some of them did join us. So our church membership began to grow. That's what I call generous encouragement.

Barnabas is an inspiring model of encouragement. Probably one of the few rich men who joined the early church in Jerusalem, he gave valuable and practical encouragement to the apostles to help people in need. He was generous too in his judgment of people. Saul after his conversion was keen to join the disciples in Jerusalem, but the disciples could only remember his previous hostility, and feared him. It was Barnabas who brought everyone together.

Later he searched out Saul (now called Paul) to join him in a teaching ministry in Antioch and beyond. Barnabas also saw potential in the young man John Mark and took him along in his mission travels when Paul would not (Acts 15.37–39). Through his giving, his words and his life of witness, Barnabas encouraged people with his generous warmth. Without him, we would not have the letters of Paul and the gospel of Mark!

Father, thank you for those who have generously encouraged me. Help me to give that same encouragement to others. Amen.

Ruth 1.15–18

'Look,' said Naomi, 'your sister-in-law is going back to her people and her gods. Go back with her.'

But Ruth replied, 'Don't urge me to leave you or to turn back from you. Where you go I will go, and where you stay I will stay. Your people will be my people and your God my God. Where you die I will die, and there I will be buried. May the LORD deal with me, be it ever so severely, if even death separates you and me.' When Naomi realized that Ruth was determined to go with her, she stopped urging her.

Ruth: Loyalty

This passage is often read at weddings and in that context it does seem quite 'mushy'. However, in the context of the book of Ruth it is incredibly profound. This declaration comes not from marital love or passion, but from loyalty alone.

Naomi and Ruth share no ancestral history, they come from different places, worship different gods and probably have a thousand and one things that they would do, think and feel differently. Ruth doesn't focus on their differences; instead, she makes this fantastic declaration of loyalty. She has the choice to go back to her familiar environment but instead she requests to stay with Naomi. She is willing to support Naomi as they venture into the unknown. She is willing to return to Naomi's hometown of Bethlehem where she will be an alien, and she chooses to trust in Naomi's God, a God unfamiliar to her past.

I find Ruth's loyalty deeply challenging. Spend a few moments and put yourself in Ruth's shoes. Ruth is likely to gain nothing from staying with Naomi; in fact she is opening herself to scrutiny and alienation and yet she remains loyal. I'm not sure that I could easily show the same loyalty and put the needs and values of another person ahead of my own.

But what if we could?

What if we were willing to go that extra mile for an unlikely relative that needs our loyalty?

Father God, help me to show loyalty like Ruth's in difficult situations; give me grace to overcome differences and support those people I know who are in real need. Amen.

[13]

Genesis 37.5–8

Joseph had a dream, and when he told it to his brothers, they hated him all the more. He said to them, 'Listen to this dream I had. We were binding sheaves of grain out in the field when suddenly my sheaf rose and stood upright, while your sheaves gathered around mine and bowed down to it.' His brothers said to him, 'Do you intend to reign over us? Will you actually rule us?' And they hated him all the more because of his dream and what he had said.

Genesis 50.18–20

His brothers then came and threw themselves down before him. 'We are your slaves,' they said. But Joseph said to them, 'Don't be afraid. Am I in the place of God? You intended to harm me, but God intended it for good to accomplish what is now being done, the saving of many lives.'

Joseph (of Genesis): Treasuring the Dream

Dreams are the stuff of aspiration, inspiration, and longing; fostering hope, carrying us into realms of imagination beyond our circumstances. Sharing dreams can be dangerous, especially when less secure people are threatened by their implications. Joseph's dream affected his family relationships, his surroundings, and his circumstances. Because of jealousy, some sought to kill the dream, but Joseph treasured it; if the dream is from God, then nothing is impossible.

For Joseph the dream-seed, charged with potential, lay invisible for a long time; but it germinated and grew, coming to fruition through experience and suffering. It led Joseph into situations beyond his control, but through trust in God Joseph developed in wisdom and patience. He learned to see the world through the hope his God-given dream gave him. It transformed defeats into opportunities, narrow escapes into reminders of God's faithfulness, trials into a divine apprenticeship for dream-fulfilment.

Perhaps you have a dream from God, one you've hidden for years. My own God-given dream has certainly felt very fragile at times, no more than a distant wisp of an unlikely idea. For years we may see no obvious progress, and our dreams may feel crushed, perhaps through periods of injustice and pain. Joseph's story encourages us to treasure and nurture God-given dreams, to trust the dream-giver and allow him to shape the dreamer. He is able to bring them to fruition in ways that are surprising and marvellous.

God, breathe upon me your inspiration; open my heart to receive your vision. Help me to depend on you as you continue to mature me, and bring your dream to fulfilment. Amen.

Mark 5.21–34

When Jesus had again crossed over by boat to the other side of the lake, a large crowd gathered around him while he was by the lake. Then one of the synagogue leaders, named Jairus, came, and when he saw Jesus, he fell at his feet. He pleaded earnestly with him, 'My little daughter is dying. Please come and put your hands on her so that she will be healed and live.' So Jesus went with him.

A large crowd followed and pressed around him. And a woman was there who had been subject to bleeding for twelve years. She had suffered a great deal under the care of many doctors and had spent all she had, yet instead of getting better she grew worse. When she heard about Jesus, she came up behind him in the crowd and touched his cloak, because she thought, 'If I just touch his clothes, I will be healed.' Immediately her bleeding stopped and she felt in her body that she was freed from her suffering.

At once Jesus realized that power had gone out from him. He turned around in the crowd and asked, 'Who touched my clothes?'

'You see the people crowding against you,' his disciples answered, 'and yet you can ask, "Who touched me?"'

But Jesus kept looking around to see who had done it. Then the woman, knowing what had happened to her, came and fell at his feet and, trembling with fear, told him the whole truth. He said to her, 'Daughter, your faith has healed you. Go in peace and be freed from your suffering.'

The Woman with the Flow of Blood: Faith to Touch Jesus

Twelve long years of suffering and pain. Twelve years of being an outcast in society, of being socially and religiously categorized as unclean and defiled, where no one would touch her in case she made them unclean. Twelve years of having hopes dashed to pieces after each doctor was unable to bring healing.

Would we dare to hope again? Would we dare to hope in being restored? In having a new life? This woman dared. How many blows can someone take before giving up completely? This woman knew all the blows – and yet when she heard about Jesus she found herself trusting in God's goodness. Even though her other attempts to be healed had only made things worse, she trusted that God would make a difference this time: 'If I just touch his clothes, I will be healed' (v.28).

This woman inspires us to believe that in reaching out to Christ we will be touched, restored and find new life. This healing might not be the kind of healing for which we have hoped, but we will be brought to a greater wholeness by the tender, and yet powerful, presence of Christ. Despite the bustle of our lives and the needs of all the people crowding around us, God knows our desire to make our way through the crowd and reach out to Christ.

Lord Jesus, thank you that when I reach out to you, you are there and do not turn away, that you want to make me whole. Help me to trust you, and to have the courage to ask to be blessed by you. Amen.

2 Samuel 11.8–11

Then David said to Uriah, 'Go down to your house and wash your feet.' So Uriah left the palace, and a gift from the king was sent after him. But Uriah slept at the entrance to the palace with all his master's servants and did not go down to his house.

David was told, 'Uriah did not go home.' So he asked Uriah, 'Haven't you just come from a military campaign? Why didn't you go home?'

Uriah said to David, 'The ark and Israel and Judah are staying in tents, and my commander Joab and my lord's men are camped in the open country. How could I go to my house to eat and drink and make love to my wife? As surely as you live, I will not do such a thing!'

Uriah the Hittite: Self-Control for the Sake of Others

While his men were fighting, David got up from his bed and went for a walk on the palace roof. The sight of Bathsheba bathing caught his wandering eyes. Within a short time, he had broken four of God's commandments by coveting, stealing, committing adultery and murder.

Uriah's actions stand in stark contrast to David's. Perhaps he suspected the king's affair with his wife from the time when David sent for him, or from David's odd request for him to stay on (2 Samuel 11.12f). By the time he was posted to fight against 'the fiercest fighters' and 'strongest defenders' at Rabbah, he may well have realized he had been sent to his own assassination.

But regardless of what he knew of David's behaviour, Uriah the Hittite (not a Hebrew) showed remarkable self-control, honouring his fellow soldiers back on the front lines and obeying the ritual law not to have intercourse whilst on military campaigns (1 Samuel 21.4–5). Even when David plied him with wine, Uriah refused to cave in to very understandable urges to sleep with his own wife.

Uriah had stunning moral clarity, saying 'no' to his natural desires to be with Bathsheba when everyone around him was urging 'yes'. His ultimate 'yes' was to God, and though his death was tragic, his example speaks powerfully to our culture today.

Heavenly Father, please grant me grace to exercise self-control for your glory and for the sake of others. Amen.

Genesis 24.15–26

Before he [Abraham's servant] had finished praying, Rebekah came out with her jar on her shoulder. She was the daughter of Bethuel son of Milkah, who was the wife of Abraham's brother Nahor. The girl was very beautiful, a virgin; no man had ever slept with her. She went down to the spring, filled her jar and came up again.

The servant hurried to meet her and said, 'Please give me a little water from your jar.'
'Drink, my lord,' she said, and quickly lowered the jar to her hands and gave him a drink.

After she had given him a drink, she said, 'I'll draw water for your camels too, until they have had enough to drink.' So she quickly emptied her jar into the trough, ran back to the well to draw more water, and drew enough for all his camels. Without saying a word, the man watched her closely to learn whether or not the LORD had made his journey successful.

When the camels had finished drinking, the man took out a gold nose ring weighing a beka and two gold bracelets weighing ten shekels. Then he asked, 'Whose daughter are you? Please tell me, is there room in your father's house for us to spend the night?'

She answered him, 'I am the daughter of Bethuel, the son that Milkah bore to Nahor.' And she added, 'We have plenty of straw and fodder, as well as room for you to spend the night.'

Then the man bowed down and worshiped the LORD.

Rebekah: Hospitality

Rebekah was going about her everyday work when she met Abraham's servant at the well. She went out of her way not only in providing water for the servant but for his camels too. She showed kindness and hospitality towards a stranger, and in the process she became an answer to a prayer.

There is an irony at the heart of this story. Rebekah wasn't expecting anything in return for showing courtesy, but through her act of simple hospitality towards another she eventually received far more than she could possibly have imagined: the gift of a husband!

Sometimes we try to create our own blessings because we think that otherwise we won't get them. We put tremendous effort into realizing our ambitions and strive to earn more in order to gain a secure and comfortable life for ourselves and our families. As our time becomes increasingly pressured, it's possible to lose the freedom to make time for others. Rebekah was looking out for the needs of a stranger and not her own, yet she was still blessed abundantly by God.

It's easy to think that by looking out for the needs of others we might miss out ourselves. But Rebekah's story shows us this isn't the case in the long run. In the smallest of tasks when we show hospitality (and especially *surprising* hospitality) others experience grace, we become answers to prayer, and people encounter something of God's love. Everyone benefits!

Father, I thank you for your many blessings. Help me to show hospitality to others today without calculating the cost or the benefits. Amen.

Acts 8.26–39

Now an angel of the Lord said to Philip, 'Go south to the road – the desert road – that goes down from Jerusalem to Gaza.' So he started out, and on his way he met an Ethiopian eunuch, an important official in charge of all the treasury of the Kandake (which means 'queen of the Ethiopians'). This man had gone to Jerusalem to worship, and on his way home was sitting in his chariot reading the Book of Isaiah the prophet. The Spirit told Philip, 'Go to that chariot and stay near it.'

Then Philip ran up to the chariot and heard the man reading Isaiah the prophet. 'Do you understand what you are reading?' Philip asked.

'How can I,' he said, 'unless someone explains it to me?' So he invited Philip to come up and sit with him . . . Then Philip began with that very passage of Scripture and told him the good news about Jesus.

As they travelled along the road, they came to some water and the eunuch said, 'Look, here is water. What can stand in the way of my being baptized?' And he gave orders to stop the chariot. Then both Philip and the eunuch went down into the water and Philip baptized him. When they came up out of the water, the Spirit of the Lord suddenly took Philip away, and the eunuch did not see him again, but went on his way rejoicing.

The Ethiopian Eunuch: The Spiritual Searcher

It's the chance encounter of the century, an evangelist's dream scenario: Philip is told by an angel to go and flag down someone's taxi. He jumps in and finds a man reading the Bible who virtually begs him to explain the good news about Jesus. Then, he's so eager to believe that he pulls in by a river and insists that Philip baptizes him on the spot. However, it's not Philip who is our hero today but the man in the chariot.

Like many people around us, the Ethiopian eunuch was on a spiritual journey. His search for truth and meaning had taken him on a long pilgrimage to one of the ancient world's major spiritual destinations, far from home. But Jerusalem had not been all that the brochure promised. As a eunuch, he was excluded from what he had set out to do – to worship in the temple (Deuteronomy 23.1). Nevertheless, he was undeterred and managed to acquire an expensive scroll by an ancient prophet. However, as he travelled home and read unfamiliar words from another time and another culture, he needed help to make sense of it all.

This man from Ethiopia is a wonderful example of someone who was actively searching for God, and in an excellent place – the scriptures. He wanted to know more, and although with his position of authority he had reason to be proud, he knew his limits and he asked for assistance.

Gracious Lord, lead me further into your word and help me to take advantage of opportunities to learn more about you. Amen.

Job 28.1–3, 9–14, 20–28

There is a mine for silver and a place where gold is refined.
Iron is taken from the earth, and copper is smelted from ore.
Miners put an end to the darkness; they search out the
farthest recesses for ore in the blackest darkness.
The miners' hands assault the flinty rock and lay bare the
roots of the mountains.
They tunnel through the rock; their eyes see all its treasures.
They search the sources of the rivers and bring hidden things
to light.
But where can wisdom be found? Where does understanding
dwell?
No mortal comprehends its worth; it cannot be found in the
land of the living.
The deep says, 'It is not in me'; the sea says, 'It is not with me.'
Where then does wisdom come from? Where does
understanding dwell?
It is hidden from the eyes of every living thing, concealed
even from the birds in the sky.
Destruction and Death say, 'Only a rumour of it has reached
our ears.'
God understands the way to it and he alone knows where it
dwells,
for he views the ends of the earth and sees everything under
the heavens.
When he established the force of the wind and measured out
the waters,
when he made a decree for the rain and a path for the
thunderstorm,
then he looked at wisdom and appraised it; he confirmed it
and tested it.
And he said to the human race, 'The fear of the Lord – that is
wisdom, and to shun evil is understanding.'

Job: Wisdom

Job was a rich man. He possessed thousands of animals and many servants. He was also a righteous man. But things went wrong for Job. He lost his family, his property, and his health. Strangely enough, people who demonstrate a saintly endurance in the face of disaster are sometimes said to have 'the patience of Job.' But Job is not patient. He complains to God; he asks questions and he wants the answers. God intervenes. In the end, Job's goods are recovered – double the amount he had before – and he has more children. Does this somehow cancel out all the suffering? Of course it doesn't.

At the heart of this book is a great poem of the achievements of humanity. At the time when the story is set, perhaps four thousand years ago, the mining of useful metals and precious stones from the depths of the earth represented the height of human technology – silver, gold, iron, copper, sapphires, jasper – 'The miners' hands assault the flinty rock and lay bare the roots of the mountains. They tunnel through the rock; their eyes see all its treasures.' People are clever and skilful. They have become wealthy through plumbing the hidden depths of the earth's resources. But are they wise? And what about Job? – is *he* wise?

'Where then does *wisdom* come from? Where does understanding dwell?' (Job 28.20).

Continuing to regard the Lord *as* Lord – *that* is wisdom. Job is wise because he stands to make his complaint before the presence of almighty God. There is no simple answer to his suffering; Job simply allows God to be God.

Be present with us, O Lord, amidst the many sufferings of this life. Help us to be wise and to continue to know you to be our loving Lord. Amen.

Luke 10.38–42

As Jesus and his disciples were on their way, he came to a village where a woman named Martha opened her home to him. She had a sister called Mary, who sat at the Lord's feet listening to what he said. But Martha was distracted by all the preparations that had to be made. She came to him and asked, 'Lord, don't you care that my sister has left me to do the work by myself? Tell her to help me!'

'Martha, Martha,' the Lord answered, 'you are worried and upset about many things, but few things are needed – or indeed only one. Mary has chosen what is better, and it will not be taken away from her.'

John 11.17–27

On his arrival, Jesus found that Lazarus had already been in the tomb for four days. Bethany was less than two miles from Jerusalem, and many Jews had come to Martha and Mary to comfort them in the loss of their brother. When Martha heard that Jesus was coming, she went out to meet him, but Mary stayed at home.

'Lord,' Martha said to Jesus, 'if you had been here, my brother would not have died. But I know that even now God will give you whatever you ask.'

Jesus said to her, 'Your brother will rise again.'

Martha answered, 'I know he will rise again in the resurrection at the last day.'

Jesus said to her, 'I am the resurrection and the life. Anyone who believes in me will live, even though they die; and whoever lives by believing in me will never die. Do you believe this?'

'Yes, Lord,' she told him, 'I believe that you are the Messiah, the Son of God, who was to come into the world.'

Martha: Practicality

It is all too easy to be overwhelmed by the practicalities of life that we are confronted with. Do we need to buy more milk? Have we paid the gas bill? These things crowd in on us and distract us from more important things, like spending time with our loved ones, talking to God and getting a good night's sleep. In the passage from Luke, Martha is the distracted and practical one, making her easy to relate to. You can imagine how she must have felt; the flurry of excitement that Jesus was coming to her house! What a frenzy of tidying, cleaning and cooking! Imagine her frustration when, exhausted by rushing around, she peeks into the room where Jesus and his disciples are sitting and sees Mary, her sister, with whom she shares her house, just sitting there doing nothing! Unsurprisingly she asks Jesus to intervene. His rebuke must have been painful: 'Don't worry about all your preparations – they're not so important. Mary's chosen the better thing.' What a bitter pill for Martha to swallow.

Of course practicality is important; but wise practicality includes learning spiritual lessons. The passage from John shows us that Martha eventually realized who and what Jesus is. She was still practical; had Jesus come earlier, Lazarus would not have died when he did! But she now had come to see that what matters most is to rely on Christ, who is there, in her grief and in her life. That practicality leads to lasting hope.

Father, in the midst of all my responsibilities, help me to learn what is practical for my spiritual life. Amen.

Nehemiah 1.1–4, 2.17, 6.15

The words of Nehemiah son of Hakaliah: In the month of
Kislev in the twentieth year, while I was in the citadel of Susa,
Hanani, one of my brothers, came from Judah with some
other men, and I questioned them about the Jewish remnant
that had survived the exile, and also about Jerusalem. They
said to me, 'Those who survived the exile and are back in the
province are in great trouble and disgrace. The wall of Jerusalem is broken down, and its gates have been burned with fire.'
When I heard these things, I sat down and wept. For some days
I mourned and fasted and prayed before the God of heaven.
Then I said to them, 'You see the trouble we are in: Jerusalem
lies in ruins, and its gates have been burned with fire. Come,
let us rebuild the wall of Jerusalem, and we will no longer be
in disgrace.' So the wall was completed on the twenty-fifth of
Elil, in fifty-two days.

Nehemiah: Faith to Rebuild

Nehemiah cared for his nation. He knew that God had made a covenant promise to Israel, one of love and dedication, but now he and his people were living in Babylon. Their past contained shameful defeat and destruction because they had not followed the Lord. They wasted so many second chances that eventually God let them face the consequences. In 587 BC, Judah was defeated by the Babylonians and taken away into exile. The few who remained in Jerusalem were an embarrassing reminder of how Nehemiah's people had taken the wrong road – the road that led away from God.

Nehemiah's example of meeting with God in prayer and then going on to face the challenge of rebuilding and renewal is inspirational. So much of human history is that of taking the path that leads away from God. The resulting tragedy takes many forms, including warring nations, poverty, broken relationships, oppression and social injustice. God does not want people to live in 'exile' and he longs to bring us back to him.

A growing number of people today are praying just as Nehemiah did, seeking guidance and asking for change. The task of renewing and rebuilding is enormous but we can make a difference, as we begin in prayer to allow God to work his purposes of renewal through us.

Father, as you worked through Nehemiah to rebuild Jerusalem, work also through me for the renewal of your world. Even though I am small, Lord, you are great. Show me the next step I can take, however small or great, for your purpose. Amen.

2 Kings 5.1–6

Now Naaman was commander of the army of the king of Aram. He was a great man in the sight of his master and highly regarded, because through him the LORD had given victory to Aram. He was a valiant soldier, but he had leprosy.

Now bands of raiders from Aram had gone out and had taken captive a young girl from Israel, and she served Naaman's wife. She said to her mistress, 'If only my master would see the prophet who is in Samaria! He would cure him of his leprosy.'

Naaman went to his master and told him what the girl from Israel had said. 'By all means, go,' the king of Aram replied. 'I will send a letter to the king of Israel.' So Naaman left, taking with him ten talents of silver, six thousand shekels of gold and ten sets of clothing. The letter that he took to the king of Israel read: 'With this letter I am sending my servant Naaman to you so that you may cure him of his leprosy.'

Naaman's Slave Girl: Daring, Faithful Compassion

A young anonymous Hebrew girl is taken to a foreign country as a slave. She ends up in the house of the army commander, the very person responsible for her being torn away from family and community. How will she respond? How would I respond, both towards God and towards the people who had captured me and expected me to serve them? Probably with anger, even despair, some doubt, and a lot of attitude!

This young girl challenges me deeply. Far from showing resentment or seeking harm for those who have enslaved her, she seeks their good. What's more, she does it with great daring. She is so confident that if Naaman will just go to see Elisha, he will be cured of his leprosy. There's no hedging of bets here. Her faith that the God of Israel would act through his prophet hasn't been diminished by her experience.

What if Naaman had not been cured? In a culture where life was cheap, the girl could have found herself in deep trouble. But she herself could not help Naaman. The only resources she had were her compassion and her God. And that compassion for an enemy and that faith in the God she served outweighed fear of personal risk. Perhaps if I had more of such selfless compassion and faith, I might be more prepared to take the risk of introducing others to Jesus Christ, who has the resources that I do not have, and who teaches us to love our enemies.

Lord Jesus, please give me the compassion I need to see others as you do, and the faith I need to trust you with them. Amen.

Luke 19.1–10

Jesus entered Jericho and was passing through. A man was there by the name of Zacchaeus; he was a chief tax collector and was wealthy. He wanted to see who Jesus was, but because he was short he could not see over the crowd. So he ran ahead and climbed a sycamore-fig tree to see him, since Jesus was coming that way.

When Jesus reached the spot, he looked up and said to him, 'Zacchaeus, come down immediately. I must stay at your house today.' So he came down at once and welcomed him gladly.

All the people saw this and began to mutter, 'He has gone to be the guest of a sinner.'

But Zacchaeus stood up and said to the Lord, 'Look, Lord! Here and now I give half of my possessions to the poor, and if I have cheated anybody out of anything, I will pay back four times the amount.'

Jesus said to him, 'Today salvation has come to this house, because this man, too, is a son of Abraham. For the Son of Man came to seek and to save what was lost.'

Zacchaeus: Curiosity

As a tax collector, Zacchaeus would have been viewed by the people of Jericho as a corrupt, money grabbing little cheat – something like a dubious second-hand car dealer today. No one would want anything to do with him. His only saving grace was that he was curious enough to try to see Jesus. We can only wonder as to his motive. Did he think there was money in it?

Maybe he was just trying to get a glimpse of Jesus without knowing what to expect. Whatever it was, his curiosity led him to climb a tree, to 'go out on a limb', to see if he could 'twig' what was going on. So he nested on a branch to get a bird's eye view – to see, but hopefully not be seen. If he was noticed by the crowd he'd become a target; some might even want to hang him from the tree.

Imagine his shock when Jesus saw him, called him by name, and honoured him by wanting to come to Zacchaeus's house for tea! His curiosity led him to a place where he could meet God in the flesh. Moved by Jesus' surprising request, he acknowledged his guilt and made a costly commitment to put right the wrongs he had done. His life was transformed.

A little curiosity can lead to wonderful discoveries. Is there any spiritual curiosity in your life? It's worth the risk to go out on a limb for a closer look at Jesus.

Father, make me curious enough to move out of my comfort zone, and teach me more about your Son. Amen.

Acts 16.13–15

On the Sabbath we went outside the city gate to the river, where we expected to find a place of prayer. We sat down and began to speak to the women who had gathered there. One of those listening was a woman from the city of Thyatira named Lydia, a dealer in purple cloth. She was a worshiper of God. The Lord opened her heart to respond to Paul's message. When she and the members of her household were baptized, she invited us to her home. 'If you consider me a believer in the Lord,' she said, 'come and stay at my house.' And she persuaded us.

Lydia: Affluent for God

I have always found Lydia an appealing character – partly because of my interest in business, partly because I like the colour purple, and partly because our daughter is called Lydia! But, above all, because of her heart, which God opened further to Jesus. When someone becomes a Christian, God has been actively involved, drawing them to respond to him.

We know that Lydia's heart was already open to some extent because Luke tells us that she was a worshipper of God before she met Paul. And the proof of her good heart is seen in the way she shared freely from her affluence. Purple cloth was a luxury item (Thyatira was known in the ancient world for its purple dye industry), and Lydia was obviously a person of means.

After she became the first European convert to Christianity, Lydia opened up her house to the travelling evangelists who had brought her the message of new life. Since the early Christians had no church buildings, they were often dependent upon the generosity of a few wealthy believers who had homes large enough for the congregations to meet in. We know from Paul's later letter to the Philippians that eventually the church that first met in Lydia's home financially supported Paul more than once in his ministry.

Despite the warnings in scripture to the rich, financial success in the world is not in opposition to a heart open to God. Sometimes less affluent Christians can be jealous, and those who are wealthy have their own temptations and issues to deal with, just as the rest of us. Lydia shows us that affluence in itself is not an evil; the question is whether one's heart is prepared to put that affluence to *God's* use.

Heavenly Father, free me from coveting what others have, and open my heart to use what you have given me for the sake of your kingdom, in Jesus' name. Amen.

Philemon 8–20

Therefore, although in Christ I could be bold and order you to do what you ought to do, yet I prefer to appeal to you on the basis of love. It is as none other than Paul – an old man and now also a prisoner of Christ Jesus – that I appeal to you for my son Onesimus, who became my son while I was in chains. Formerly he was useless to you, but now he has become useful both to you and to me.

I am sending him – who is my very heart – back to you. I would have liked to keep him with me so that he could take your place in helping me while I am in chains for the gospel. But I did not want to do anything without your consent, so that any favour you do would not seem forced but would be voluntary. Perhaps the reason he was separated from you for a little while was that you might have him back forever – no longer as a slave, but better than a slave, as a dear brother. He is very dear to me but even dearer to you, both as a fellow man and as a brother in the Lord.

So if you consider me a partner, welcome him as you would welcome me. If he has done you any wrong or owes you anything, charge it to me. I, Paul, am writing this with my own hand. I will pay it back – not to mention that you owe me your very self. I do wish, brother, that I may have some benefit from you in the Lord; refresh my heart in Christ. Confident of your obedience, I write to you, knowing that you will do even more than I ask.

Onesimus: Useful

I can imagine young Onesimus sitting in the slaves' quarters of Philemon's house in Asia Minor grumbling and threatening to run away, threats that were not taken too seriously. Maybe it was still dark when the slave crept out and embarked on a search for freedom.

Onesimus was seeking help and perhaps advocacy from someone he knew his master Philemon respected – Paul, who was under house arrest awaiting trial. Paul drew him under his wing; through the apostle's care and conversation, Onesimus came to faith. The little Letter to Philemon is Paul persuading Philemon to welcome the runaway back, now much more than a slave – as a brother in Christ.

Paul plays on words: 'Onesimus' means 'Useful'. As he points out, until now the young man has hardly lived up to his name. However, a transformation has taken place in the slave's life, and 'now he is useful to you *and* to me.' Paul hopes that Philemon will release Onesimus to return to the apostle to serve freely without threat of reprisal. A fearful man whose life looked like a failure turned out to be of real help to others.

Some fifty years later a man named Onesimus was the bishop of Ephesus. Was this the same person? We don't know for sure. But what we do know is that wherever we go, God's transforming grace pursues us. There is no reason why the runaway who took a big risk should not one day have become an influential Christian leader, mentor, and guide.

Lord God, make me useful in your service. In Jesus' name, Amen.

Genesis 32.22–32

That night Jacob got up and took his two wives, his two female servants and his eleven sons and crossed the ford of the Jabbok. After he had sent them across the stream, he sent over all his possessions. So Jacob was left alone, and a man wrestled with him till daybreak. When the man saw that he could not overpower him, he touched the socket of Jacob's hip so that his hip was wrenched as he wrestled with the man. Then the man said, 'Let me go, for it is daybreak.'

But Jacob replied, 'I will not let you go unless you bless me.'

The man asked him, 'What is your name?'

'Jacob,' he answered.

Then the man said, 'Your name will no longer be Jacob, but Israel, because you have struggled with God and with human beings and have overcome.'

Jacob said, 'Please tell me your name.'

But he replied, 'Why do you ask my name?' Then he blessed him there.

So Jacob called the place Peniel, saying, 'It is because I saw God face to face, and yet my life was spared.'

The sun rose above him as he passed Peniel, and he was limping because of his hip. Therefore to this day the Israelites do not eat the tendon attached to the socket of the hip, because the socket of Jacob's hip was touched near the tendon.

Jacob: God's Rascal

It is hard to find one word that best describes Jacob, so 'scoundrel' and 'rascal' are two that work well for me! He was a twister who spent his earlier years getting his own way by scamming those around him, including his elder brother, Esau, whose birthright he stole. He discovered swindling was a family trait when he fled from Esau, went into business with his uncle, Laban, and found himself on the receiving end of a real pro!

Finally Jacob managed to give Laban a taste of his own medicine. He then headed home, only to discover Esau was coming to meet him. After taking appropriate precautions, he spent the night alone at Peniel and found himself in a life and death struggle with the angel of God. He walked away from the encounter with a new name and a limp, and his life would never be the same again. At Peniel, he found out that the Almighty cannot be double-crossed.

Despite Jacob's flawed character, God still wanted to wrestle with him. That night at Peniel became a turning point. We may not see ourselves wrestling with God, but there are other battles that leave their scars. Yet, in the midst of those battles, God is at work in our lives in ways that we may not always understand, or necessarily want, shaping us to be the people he wants us to be, just as he did with Jacob.

Teach me, Lord God, to bear the scars of struggles in the pilgrim path of this earthly life as your Son bore his, for the sake of your name. Amen.

1 Samuel 1.1–3, 9–18

There was a certain man from Ramathaim . . . whose name was Elkanah . . . He had two wives; one was called Hannah and the other Peninnah. Peninnah had children, but Hannah had none. Year after year this man went up from his town to worship and sacrifice to the LORD Almighty at Shiloh . . . Once when they had finished eating and drinking in Shiloh, Hannah stood up. Now Eli the priest was sitting on a chair by the doorpost of the LORD's temple. In bitterness of soul Hannah wept much and prayed to the LORD. And she made a vow, saying, 'O LORD Almighty, if you will only look upon your servant's misery and remember me, and not forget your servant but give her a son, then I will give him to the LORD for all the days of his life, and no razor will ever be used on his head.'

As she kept on praying to the LORD, Eli observed her mouth. Hannah was praying in her heart, and her lips were moving but her voice was not heard. Eli thought she was drunk and said to her, 'How long will you keep on getting drunk? Get rid of your wine.'

'Not so, my lord,' Hannah replied, 'I am a woman who is deeply troubled. I have not been drinking wine or beer; I was pouring out my soul to the LORD. Do not take your servant for a wicked woman; I have been praying here out of my great anguish and grief.' Eli answered, 'Go in peace, and may the God of Israel grant you what you have asked of him.'

She said, 'May your servant find favour in your eyes.' Then she went her way and ate something, and her face was no longer downcast.

Early the next morning they arose and worshiped before the LORD and then went back to their home at Ramah. Elkanah made love to his wife Hannah, and the LORD remembered her. So in the course of time Hannah became pregnant and gave birth to a son. She named him Samuel, saying, 'Because I asked the LORD for him.'

Hannah: Praying in Disappointment

Expectations disappointed, hopes unrealized; a sense of failure and disgrace. Our own lives may contain echoes of Hannah's pain. How do we respond to disappointment? My friend and her husband hope to have children, yet each pregnancy ends in miscarriage. In the face of unanswerable questions, she has felt forgotten by God and has gradually distanced herself from him.

Hannah's response to disappointment was to pour out her soul to the Lord. As she brought her pain from the darkness of her soul into the light of his presence she gradually saw her situation differently. She began to see herself from God's perspective and to sense something of God's purposes for her. Her prayer was transformed from asking for what she lacked into giving what she hoped to gain.

My friend has recently brought her own grief to God, and reflects that ' . . . it all matters a lot less in the light of the bigger picture.' She explains, 'I've been stamping my foot about my wants and desires without recognizing his, and that's left me feeling isolated.' She, like Hannah, has glimpsed the bigger picture and says, 'God wants me to be a colour in it, which brings me peace'.

Hannah wanted to be the mother of a son to take away her shame. God wanted her to be the mother of a son – who would hear his voice, a prophet who would anoint kings – to take away the shame of his people.

Heavenly Father, when I feel distant from you or bitter, give me grace to bring my pain to you and to discover your perspective. Amen.

1 Samuel 14.1–2, 3b–15

One day Jonathan son of Saul said to his young armour-bearer, 'Come, let's go over to the Philistine outpost on the other side.' But he did not tell his father.

No one was aware that Jonathan had left. On each side of the pass that Jonathan intended to cross to reach the Philistine outpost was a cliff; one was called Bozez and the other Seneh. One cliff stood to the north toward Mikmash, the other to the south toward Geba.

Jonathan said to his young armour-bearer, 'Come, let's go over to the outpost of those uncircumcised fellows. Perhaps the LORD will act in our behalf. Nothing can hinder the LORD from saving, whether by many or by few.' 'Do all that you have in mind,' his armour-bearer said. 'Go ahead; I am with you heart and soul.' Jonathan said, 'Come on, then; we will cross over toward them and let them see us. If they say to us, "Wait there until we come to you," we will stay where we are and not go up to them. But if they say, "Come up to us," we will climb up, because that will be our sign that the LORD has given them into our hands.' So both of them showed themselves to the Philistine outpost. 'Look!' said the Philistines. 'The Hebrews are crawling out of the holes they were hiding in.' The men of the outpost shouted to Jonathan and his armour-bearer, 'Come up to us and we'll teach you a lesson.' So Jonathan said to his armour-bearer, 'Climb up after me; the LORD has given them into the hand of Israel.' Jonathan climbed up, using his hands and feet, with his armour-bearer right behind him. The Philistines fell before Jonathan, and his armour-bearer followed and killed behind him. In that first attack Jonathan and his armour-bearer killed some twenty men in an area of about half an acre. Then panic struck the whole army – those in the camp and field, and those in the outposts and raiding parties – and the ground shook. It was a panic sent by God.

Jonathan: Daring Bravery

Jonathan and his father King Saul, campaigning against the Philistines, found themselves in an impasse. The enemy had encamped in a strategic cliff top position. Down in the valley the generals had no plan, the army sat silent and the priest had no words from God. So the King, like all good bureaucrats, called a committee meeting and played for time.

Meanwhile, Jonathan quietly slipped away with his armour-bearer to tackle the issue. Taking the bull by the horns he declared, 'Perhaps the LORD will act in our behalf.'

Was he courageous or impetuous? Is this daring action or an unnecessary risk? Did he presume on the will of God or blindly act on instinct? Jonathan's reasoning for his bold move is filled with doggedness, faith and determination, 'Nothing can hinder the LORD from saving, whether by many or by few.'

Jonathan knew that God was more powerful than the Philistines. This knowledge motivated him and his armour-bearer to tenacious action. Moving towards the enemy they waited for a sign. When the Philistines jeered and called them up, the two-man army saw God's green light. Outnumbered ten to one, Jonathan and the armour-bearer steadily climbed up to their foes, and took them on. By surprise, skill and God's sovereignty they were unstoppable. Panic ensued, God roared and the enemy was routed!

When faced with an insurmountable issue I am encouraged by Jonathan's daring example. *Sometimes* in God's service, we need to take a risk, rather than wait for directions from a committee.

Lord, help me to know your will, follow your lead and be intrepid in my commitment to you. Amen.

2 Timothy 1.1–7

Paul, an apostle of Christ Jesus by the will of God, in keeping with the promise of life that is in Christ Jesus,

To Timothy, my dear son:

Grace, mercy and peace from God the Father and Christ Jesus our Lord.

I thank God, whom I serve, as my ancestors did, with a clear conscience, as night and day I constantly remember you in my prayers. Recalling your tears, I long to see you, so that I may be filled with joy. I am reminded of your sincere faith, which first lived in your grandmother Lois and in your mother Eunice and, I am persuaded, now lives in you also.

For this reason I remind you to fan into flame the gift of God, which is in you through the laying on of my hands. For the Spirit God gave us does not make us timid, but gives us power, love and self-discipline.

Timothy: Strength in Weakness

We meet 'Timid Timothy' first in Acts 16.1 where the apostle Paul takes him from his home town of Lystra and commissions him for missionary work. The son of a believing Jewish mother, Eunice, he seems to have been a remarkably frail character. We know from 1 & 2 Timothy that he was prone to illness, and although gifted, weak in confidence. Nevertheless, he led the struggling and deeply divided church at Ephesus. There seem to be so many things in Timothy's life that threaten an effective ministry – sickness, a timid nature and opposition.

In my own Christian life I often feel weak and nowhere near up to the task of staying faithful to Jesus. I find it hard enough just to fend off a common cold! I'm too timid to be useful in the Lord's service. I'm far too weak to stand up to opposition to the gospel. But it's exactly in these times of weakness that I can learn from Timothy; because he was weak and not up to the task, he knew it was only in the power of God's Spirit that he could do anything. He relied on the Spirit's power to keep going in the face of opposition. He relied on the Spirit of love to enable him to be gracious towards those who disagreed with him. He relied on the Spirit of self control, to live a godly life in an ungodly culture.

Loving Father, thank you that you have chosen the weak things of the world to shame the strong, that you use 'Timid Timothys' in your service. Thank you for the gift of your Spirit in me. Amen.

Matthew 1.20, 24

An angel of the Lord appeared to him in a dream and said,
'Joseph son of David, do not be afraid to take Mary home as
your wife, because what is conceived in her is from the Holy
Spirit.' When Joseph woke up, he did what the angel of the
Lord had commanded him.

Joseph of Nazareth: A Trustworthy Dreamer

Dreamers get a bad press. They're generally reckoned dozy or lazy, not much use. But what people do with their dreams makes all the difference.

We're told very little about Joseph, the earthly father of Jesus – he was from Nazareth and he was a builder. He was also a trustworthy man who followed the dreams God gave him. For Joseph, dreams were a way by which God spoke to him. Urgent dreams, practical dreams, dreams that told him the will of God: 'Do not be afraid to take Mary home as your wife' (Matthew 1.20). 'Get up, take the child and escape' (2.13). 'Get up and return to the land of Israel' (2.20). And, finally, he was 'warned in a dream' not to go back to Judea (2.22). Joseph obeyed God. He did the right thing by Mary and protected the child God had entrusted to him.

With that Joseph disappears from history, apart from the story of his concern when the boy Jesus stayed behind at the temple (Luke 2.41–51). But God's plan needed him and his steady reliability just as much as it needed Mary's willingness to 'let it be with me according to your word'. His role may look almost like a walk-on part, but without it the rest of Jesus' story couldn't have happened.

Joseph trusted God, even when it risked bringing shame or disgrace in the eyes of some. His story challenges us to listen for God's voice, to follow, and to see wonderful things result.

Father, thank you for Joseph's trustworthiness and obedience to your word. Help me to hear, recognize and obey your voice. Amen.

Daniel 3.13–20, 24–26

Furious with rage, Nebuchadnezzar summoned Shadrach, Meshach and Abednego. So these men were brought before the king, and Nebuchadnezzar said to them, 'Is it true, Shadrach, Meshach and Abednego, that you do not serve my gods or worship the image of gold I have set up? Now when you hear the sound of the horn, flute, zither, lyre, harp, pipe and all kinds of music, if you are ready to fall down and worship the image I made, very good. But if you do not worship it, you will be thrown immediately into a blazing furnace. Then what god will be able to rescue you from my hand?'

Shadrach, Meshach and Abednego replied to him, 'King Nebuchadnezzar, we do not need to defend ourselves before you in this matter. If the God we serve is able to deliver us, then he will deliver us from the blazing furnace and from Your Majesty's hand. But even if he does not, we want you to know, Your Majesty, that we will not serve your gods or worship the image of gold you have set up.'

Then Nebuchadnezzar was furious with Shadrach, Meshach and Abednego, and his attitude toward them changed. He ordered the furnace heated seven times hotter than usual and commanded some of the strongest soldiers in his army to tie up Shadrach, Meshach and Abednego and throw them into the blazing furnace.

. . . Then King Nebuchadnezzar leaped to his feet in amazement and asked his advisers, 'Weren't there three men that we tied up and threw into the fire?'

They replied, 'Certainly, Your Majesty.' He said, 'Look! I see four men walking around in the fire, unbound and unharmed, and the fourth looks like a son of the gods.' Nebuchadnezzar then approached the opening of the blazing furnace and shouted, 'Shadrach, Meshach and Abednego, servants of the Most High God, come out! Come here!'

Shadrach, Meshach and Abednego: Standing Firm

Shadrach, Meshach and Abednego are three courageous and determined characters in the book of Daniel who stand up for what they believe and are willing to face the resulting fire.

They refuse to bow down before a golden image of a god, because they know that there is only one true God whom they worship and serve. They are unwilling to compromise. They don't try to explain away their actions when confronted by a man with the power to hurt them – the Babylonian king Nebuchadnezzar. Shadrach, Meshach and Abednego merely state their faith and trust in God. In their minds it is a simple choice: 'we trust God and will serve him only'. They stake their lives on God. In the face of adversity they will not be swayed from their stance.

In the West we don't normally have our life threatened because of our faith (although many Christians do face that danger elsewhere), but at times it can cost us to stand up for the truth. Shadrach, Meshach and Abednego remind us to act with integrity and not to compromise even when a faithful choice will cost us dearly.

Many Christians throughout the ages have stood firm for the Gospel in obedience to God. We may not be called to be a William Tyndale, William Wilberforce, Martin Luther King or Mother Teresa, but when we are confronted with pressure to compromise, how do we respond? The challenge for us is to be able to see clearly which issues require a stand, and how to do so in a way that conveys God's character.

Lord, give me wisdom to know when to take a strong stand and how to do so for your glory, Amen.

Esther 4.1, 15–17

When Mordecai learned of all that had been done, he tore his clothes, put on sackcloth and ashes, and went out into the city, wailing loudly and bitterly . . .

Then Esther sent this reply to Mordecai: 'Go, gather together all the Jews who are in Susa, and fast for me. Do not eat or drink for three days, night or day. I and my attendants will fast as you do. When this is done, I will go to the king, even though it is against the law. And if I perish, I perish.'

So Mordecai went away and carried out all of Esther's instructions.

Esther: Fasting

Esther was a beautiful orphaned Hebrew girl living as a captive in the land of Persia, where her people had been carried away in the sixth century BC. She was selected by the Persian king to be queen of the whole Empire. When a plot was hatched by one of the king's officials to kill all the Jews in the land, Esther directed the Jews to observe a fast. She then bravely spoke out to the king – an action for which she could have been executed – about the plight of her people. Their destiny was changed and the people were delivered.

I come from a Hindu family, some of whom are used to fasting as part of their religious devotion. When I first came to faith in Christ I tried it simply to show my family that Christ, too, took fasting seriously. In spite of my dubious motives, God brought blessing and soon after I was able to be baptized and confirmed.

Lent is traditionally a time for change – for fasting, reprioritizing and getting our focus back on the Lord and the things he cares about. Today, God is looking for people like Esther who want change seriously enough to fast as well as to pray for it. He is searching for those who will share his concern and love for the poor, the persecuted, the broken and lost, and who will pray, fast, and act to see God's liberating power. Have you discovered the power of fasting – not for your own benefit, but for someone else's?

Heavenly Father, thank you for moving Esther to fast and pray and act to see things change. Help me to do the same for your kingdom. Amen.

John 20.19–29

On the evening of that first day of the week, when the disciples were together, with the doors locked for fear of the Jewish leaders, Jesus came and stood among them and said, 'Peace be with you!' After he said this, he showed them his hands and side. The disciples were overjoyed when they saw the Lord.

Again Jesus said, 'Peace be with you! As the Father has sent me, I am sending you.' And with that he breathed on them and said, 'Receive the Holy Spirit. If you forgive the sins of anyone, their sins are forgiven; if you do not forgive them, they are not forgiven.'

Now Thomas (also known as Didymus), one of the Twelve, was not with the disciples when Jesus came. So the other disciples told him, 'We have seen the Lord!'

But he said to them, 'Unless I see the nail marks in his hands and put my finger where the nails were, and put my hand into his side, I will not believe.'

A week later his disciples were in the house again, and Thomas was with them. Though the doors were locked, Jesus came and stood among them and said, 'Peace be with you!' Then he said to Thomas, 'Put your finger here; see my hands. Reach out your hand and put it into my side. Stop doubting and believe.'

Thomas said to him, 'My Lord and my God!'

Then Jesus told him, 'Because you have seen me, you have believed; blessed are those who have not seen and yet have believed.'

Thomas: Transformed Doubt

'Doubting Thomas!' A harsh nickname following a moment of uncertainty during the worst week of his life. It's easy to have an unfavourable impression of Thomas. The other disciples had all seen Jesus risen, alive and speaking. Thomas hadn't and he simply couldn't trust the witness of his friends.

But Thomas had an analytical mind; there is a refreshing and honest realism about him. He had realized the dangers of returning to Jerusalem (John 11.7–16) and, to his credit, wasn't afraid to ask questions when he didn't understand (John 14.5). And now he wanted real evidence. How could he believe that Jesus, his teacher, friend and hero, was alive again without actually seeing him first-hand?

The vital fact is that he chose to return to the house with the disciples when he still had so many unanswered questions. He kept meeting with them. Perhaps he had learned enough about Jesus to dare to hope that there could be more to learn. Eventually it paid off. When he finally met his risen Lord his doubt was transformed into the supreme confession in John's Gospel. What a turn-around!

It's only natural to have questions and Jesus knows that belief in him today will be no easy matter. From Thomas we can learn the value of keeping company with Christ's followers. Even the most deep-seated doubt can be transformed into a powerful witness by Jesus' presence experienced with his people.

By grace, Thomas' decision to stay led to faith enabling him to proclaim Jesus not just as his friend and teacher, but as his Lord and his God. Yet even more blessed are those who believe without seeing.

Lord Jesus, give me the eyes of faith to trust you with my questions and encounter you among your people. Amen.

Mark 7.24–30

Jesus left that place and went to the vicinity of Tyre. He entered a house and did not want anyone to know it; yet he could not keep his presence secret. In fact, as soon as she heard about him, a woman whose little daughter was possessed by an evil spirit came and fell at his feet. The woman was a Greek, born in Syrian Phoenicia. She begged Jesus to drive the demon out of her daughter.

'First let the children eat all they want,' he told her, 'for it is not right to take the children's bread and toss it to the dogs.'

'Lord,' she replied, 'even the dogs under the table eat the children's crumbs.'

Then he told her, 'For such a reply, you may go; the demon has left your daughter.'

She went home and found her child lying on the bed, and the demon gone.

The Syro-Phoenician Woman: Ingenuity

It's hard to appreciate just how many barriers the Syro-Phoenician woman has to crash through here to get help for her daughter.

As a woman, she would be considered socially inferior to men and shouldn't initiate such a conversation. As a Gentile she would differ in her ideas about belief and behaviour, and Jews generally avoided contact with such people for fear of becoming unclean; she risks immediate rejection in approaching Jesus.

Jesus seems to confirm her worst fears. In the unflattering contrast between children and dogs he tells her he has come for the Jews; as a Gentile she has no right to expect his help. She could well be offended and give up, but instead she chooses to argue. She concedes the basic point, but in a move that Jesus would admire she offers a creative response. It's a humble but witty reply, as she picks up his image and develops it, turning his argument back on him. She believes Jesus can heal her daughter, and she skilfully gets her prayer answered.

I admire the pluck, humility and ingenuity of this woman. She inspires me to push against the barriers and to speak out more boldly in situations when it would be easier to give up. She also motivates me to persist in prayer; engaging in real, passionate dialogue with God about the things that matter to me. Jesus isn't offended by robust dialogue!

Lord, help me to persevere in prayer with you about things that really matter. Give me courage to speak out on behalf of others in spite of barriers that stand in the way, for your glory. Amen.

1 Samuel 25.3b, 14–15, 17–20, 23–24

She [Abigail] was an intelligent and beautiful woman, but her husband was surly and mean in his dealings.

One of the servants told Abigail, Nabal's wife, 'David sent messengers from the wilderness to give our master his greetings, but he hurled insults at them. Yet these men were very good to us. They did not mistreat us, and the whole time we were out in the fields near them nothing was missing. Now think it over and see what you can do, because disaster is hanging over our master and his whole household. He is such a wicked man that no one can talk to him.' Abigail acted quickly. She took two hundred loaves of bread, two skins of wine, five dressed sheep, five seahs of roasted grain, a hundred cakes of raisins and two hundred cakes of pressed figs, and loaded them on donkeys. Then she told her servants, 'Go on ahead; I'll follow you.' But she did not tell her husband Nabal. As she came riding her donkey into a mountain ravine, there were David and his men descending toward her, and she met them.

When Abigail saw David, she quickly got off her donkey and bowed down before David with her face to the ground. She fell at his feet and said: 'Pardon your servant, my lord, and let me speak to you; hear what your servant has to say . . . '

Abigail: Courageous Wisdom

Imagine going out to meet four hundred armed men trained in battle who have one mission in mind – to pay back the insults heaped on them by your husband. Abigail did this.

Imagine having to work behind the back of your mean and surly husband to bring reconciliation and save the lives of your household. Abigail did this.

Imagine falling on your knees in front of a king and humbly apologizing for your husband's actions. Abigail did this.

Imagine having that courageous wisdom of knowing when and how to act, with grace and humility, with no second plans or escape routes. Abigail had this.

Abigail is a surprisingly little known character from the Old Testament, but her actions are gracious and show great courage in the face of danger, great wisdom in the face of folly. Often in our church and society we are timid and fail to prevent avoidable suffering; we hesitate to step forward and we fail to take action; we are proud and fail to apologize humbly for our own mistakes or for those we represent. Abigail, however, gives us hope. She reminds us that whoever we are, whatever situation we are in, whatever background we have, we can aspire to be courageous and wise, without foolishness or arrogance. With bold tact and diplomacy we too, in the footsteps of Abigail, can begin to reconcile broken situations and create new beginnings.

Almighty God, help me to speak and act with courageous wisdom, so that I may uphold goodness and peace within my family and society. Amen.

Luke 1.26–38

God sent the angel Gabriel to Nazareth, a town in Galilee, to a virgin pledged to be married to a man named Joseph, a descendant of David. The virgin's name was Mary. The angel went to her and said,

'Greetings, you who are highly favoured! The Lord is with you.'

Mary was greatly troubled at his words and wondered what kind of greeting this might be. But the angel said to her, 'Do not be afraid, Mary, you have found favour with God. You will conceive and give birth to a son, and you are to call him Jesus. He will be great and will be called the Son of the Most High. The Lord God will give him the throne of his father David, and he will reign over the house of Jacob forever; his kingdom will never end.'

'How will this be,' Mary asked the angel, 'since I am a virgin?'

The angel answered, 'The Holy Spirit will come on you, and the power of the Most High will overshadow you. So the holy one to be born will be called the Son of God.' . . .

'I am the Lord's servant,' Mary answered. 'May it be to me according to your word.' Then the angel left her.

Mary the Mother of Jesus: Saying 'Yes' to God

If you ever have the opportunity to visit Ridley Hall chapel you'll see that it is flanked with a variety of stained glass windows; on the left are the early church Fathers and on the right are the Reformers. But the only woman who makes an appearance in the chapel windows is Mary, the mother of Jesus. She is placed in a tiny but rather beautiful section of the East window listening to the angel Gabriel according to our story opposite. The window catches the characters in action as the angel addresses Mary in those famous words. After initially questioning Gabriel, Mary accepts her vocation, saying 'I am the Lord's servant . . . may it be to me according to your word.'

Throughout Luke's Gospel, Mary is portrayed as a model disciple. She is truly one of those who, as Jesus says, 'hears the word of God and obeys it' (Luke 11.28). Mary is present at the major events in the life of her son, even at his crucifixion. Of course Mary had a unique vocation to be the mother of our Lord, but in Mary's 'yes' we too are invited to echo her simple acceptance. Some days it seems easy to say 'yes' to God, but more often than not we say it through gritted teeth. Yet if we say 'yes' to God, it will bring us closer to Jesus as it did with Mary, even though it may bring suffering. So may her 'yes' in bearing Christ to the world also become our 'yes' as we seek to do the same.

Father, help me by your grace to follow Mary's example in saying 'yes' to you, carrying Christ into your world. Amen.

Hosea 1.1–3; 2.19–20

The word of the LORD that came to Hosea son of Beeri during the reigns of Uzziah, Jotham, Ahaz and Hezekiah, kings of Judah, and during the reign of Jeroboam son of Jehoash [a] king of Israel:

When the LORD began to speak through Hosea, the LORD said to him, 'Go, marry a promiscuous woman and have children with her, for like an adulterous wife this land is guilty of unfaithfulness to the LORD.' So he married Gomer daughter of Diblaim, and she conceived and bore him a son.

I will betroth you to me forever;
I will betroth you in righteousness and justice,
in love and compassion.
I will betroth you in faithfulness,
and you will acknowledge the LORD.

Hosea: Faithfulness

What kind of partner do you desire? Faithful, committed, in for the long haul? If your answer is yes, then Hosea is your man and Hosea's God is your God.

The unfaithfulness, adultery and prostitution of Hosea's wife tested the limits of this man's faithfulness, but did not destroy it. He bought his wife, brought her out of a life of prostitution and wooed her back to himself.

Hosea's experience was a prophetic sign or an acted parable of the commitment of God to his adulterous and rebellious people. God chose Israel and bound himself to her in a covenant. Israel was to be a nation living in faithful, committed relationship to the God who had chosen her and demonstrated his love for the people so powerfully throughout their history.

Israel had promised to worship him alone, but her response to God's love had been 'like a morning cloud, like the dew that goes away early' (6.4). She left him for the Canaanite gods. Hosea's faithfulness to his wayward wife reflected God's yearning heart that promised, 'I will heal their disloyalty; I will love them freely, for my anger has turned from them . . . They shall again live beneath my shadow' (14.4, 7).

I sometimes falter like Israel and am tempted to turn my back on God. Hosea's faithfulness reminds me of God's unchanging love for me – even when I fail – and challenges me to act with grace towards those who disappoint me.

Father, I thank you that you are a faithful and forgiving God. May my love for you and for others be full of that same faithfulness and forgiveness. Amen.

Matthew 20.20–28

Then the mother of Zebedee's sons came to Jesus with her sons and, kneeling down, asked a favour of him. 'What is it you want?' he asked. She said, 'Grant that one of these two sons of mine may sit at your right and the other at your left in your kingdom.' 'You don't know what you are asking,' Jesus said to them. 'Can you drink the cup I am going to drink?' 'We can,' they answered. Jesus said to them, 'You will indeed drink from my cup, but to sit at my right or left is not for me to grant. These places belong to those for whom they have been prepared by my Father.'

When the ten heard about this, they were indignant with the two brothers. Jesus called them together and said, 'You know that the rulers of the Gentiles lord it over them, and their high officials exercise authority over them. Not so with you. Instead, whoever wants to become great among you must be your servant, and whoever wants to be first must be your slave – just as the Son of Man did not come to be served, but to serve, and to give his life as a ransom for many.'

Mrs Zebedee: A Mother's Courage

Mrs Zebedee's boys want something big from Jesus but are apparently afraid to ask. So this woman who seeks the best for her children kneels before Jesus to ask for them what no one would dare. To sit at Jesus' right and left in his kingdom meant places of the highest honour. Answering, Jesus addresses the brothers: he knows the question is really their own. He does not rebuke them, but promises only that they will 'share his cup.'

The other disciples are outraged at this jockeying for position, so things turn stormy for the 'Sons of Thunder'. Jesus gently corrects all twelve. In God's topsy-turvy kingdom, the leader will serve; the strongest will give his life to save others. James, John and the others must learn this new kind of ambition. Before the cup of the new wine of the kingdom comes the cup of suffering.

Both of Mrs Zebedee's sons went on to gain high honour, although not in the way she imagined. James was the first of the twelve disciples to experience martyrdom (Acts 12.2), and his brother John had the honour of caring for our Lord's mother and writing the Fourth Gospel. Mrs Zebedee may have been embarrassed by Jesus' gentle correction of her well-meant but mistaken prayer, but that did not keep her from persevering. Long after the disciples scattered for fear of their lives, this woman of courage stayed close to Jesus even at the site of his crucifixion (Matt. 27:55–56).

Lord, help me to bring my heart's desires to you with honesty, and to stay close to you today and to the end of my life's journey. Amen.

Mark 12.41–44

Jesus sat down opposite the place where the offerings were put and watched the crowd putting their money into the temple treasury. Many rich people threw in large amounts. But a poor widow came and put in two very small copper coins, worth only a fraction of a penny.

Calling his disciples to him, Jesus said, 'I tell you the truth, this poor widow has put more into the treasury than all the others. They all gave out of their wealth; but she, out of her poverty, put in everything – all she had to live on.'

The Widow Who Gave the Most: A Generous Heart

We know so little about this widow, only that Jesus noticed her and was impressed by her generosity. She would have been an insignificant member of society, poor and totally dependent on her relatives and the charity of others, but she gave all that she had. She could have withheld her gift and rationalized that decision by considering how it might be misspent by the temple authorities, but she gave it to God anyway. Like the woman who anointed Jesus' feet with expensive perfume, she will always be remembered; this part of her story will always be told.

In my early teens I was in hospital and while I was there I met a young woman with cerebral palsy. She would never walk, and her limbs, in particular her arms and hands, were twisted from contracted muscles; she was often in discomfort. However she was always cheerful and spent much of her time slowly and painfully knitting squares that would be sewn into blankets for children in the third world. In the extreme poverty of her physical circumstances her concern was not for herself but for others. Like the widow, that young woman must have had a grateful and generous heart to give so much when she appeared to have so little.

Whatever and whenever we give, God takes notice. He knows our circumstances and what it costs us. We are created in the image of a giving God, and he delights when we reflect his own costly self-giving.

Heavenly Father, remind me afresh of how much you have given me, and help me to discover the joy of giving generously. Amen.

John 6.5–14

When Jesus looked up and saw a great crowd coming toward him, he said to Philip, 'Where shall we buy bread for these people to eat?' He asked this only to test him, for he already had in mind what he was going to do.

Philip answered him, 'It would take almost a year's wages to buy enough bread for each one to have a bite!'

Another of his disciples, Andrew, Simon Peter's brother, spoke up, 'Here is a boy with five small barley loaves and two small fish, but how far will they go among so many?'

Jesus said, 'Have the people sit down.' There was plenty of grass in that place, and they sat down (about five thousand men were there). Jesus then took the loaves, gave thanks, and distributed to those who were seated as much as they wanted. He did the same with the fish.

When they had all had enough to eat, he said to his disciples, 'Gather the pieces that are left over. Let nothing be wasted.' So they gathered them and filled twelve baskets with the pieces of the five barley loaves left over by those who had eaten.

After the people saw the sign Jesus performed, they began to say, 'Surely this is the Prophet who is to come into the world.'

The Boy with the Loaves and Fishes: Insignificance

Buried deep in John's account of this well-known story is a small and seemingly insignificant detail. John alone tells us who provided the loaves and fishes. Amongst the great crowd that was packed onto the mountainside that day, there was a small boy carrying his packed lunch.

Though the text doesn't say, I have always imagined the boy on the fringe of the crowd, literally as well as figuratively on the sidelines – an insignificant spectator among much more important people. As a boy, his value and worth to his family and society was in his future rather than anything he could offer to them now. Only when he eventually grew to physical maturity and could work and earn money would he have something to contribute to his family and his community. His meagre rations of the cheapest bread and small, pickled fish tell of a boy from the poorest of circumstances. This was not someone the world was going to notice.

Yet, through the willingness of a child that the world had no time for, Jesus was able to feed a multitude and work a great miracle. This boy did nothing more than turn up and hold out what little he had as an offering for Jesus to use; in doing so he models our own faith in Christ. He had little; but in the hands of Jesus, what he was willing to share was multiplied far beyond his imagination.

Dear Lord, open my eyes to the 'insignificant' people I know whose offerings may seem meagre and unworthy. Multiply the blessings that come in those who are overlooked but willing to share what they have. Amen.

1 Chronicles 11.22–25

Benaiah son of Jehoiada, a valiant fighter from Kabzeel, performed great exploits. He struck down Moab's two mightiest
warriors. He also went down into a pit on a snowy day and
killed a lion. And he struck down an Egyptian who was five
cubits tall. Although the Egyptian had a spear like a weaver's
rod in his hand, Benaiah went against him with a club. He
snatched the spear from the Egyptian's hand and killed him
with his own spear. Such were the exploits of Benaiah son of
Jehoiada; he too was as famous as the three mighty warriors.
He was held in greater honour than any of the Thirty, but
he was not included among the Three. And David put him in
charge of his bodyguard.

Benaiah: Second Best?

Benaiah was one of King David's thirty mighty men who fought alongside him and protected him. We're told he defeated a lion, and killed a seven-and-a-half-foot giant with his own spear. Yet, despite Benaiah's exploits, he was not considered one of 'the Three' – those who were the mightiest of all (2 Sam 23.8–11). He shared equal fame, but wasn't included among them. Compared to them, Benaiah could be described as second best.

In life we work hard and try to accomplish as much as we can, but no matter how much recognition we might receive there will always be someone who does it better. I look around at my fellow ordinands and long for his beautiful speaking voice or for her academic skills, and one day I may make the mistake of comparing their congregations to mine. But God does not require that we are the best at everything. We may not be included in the top award winners; what matters is doing whatever we're called to do with the best of our abilities and leaving the praise to God.

Benaiah was made the leader of David's royal bodyguard and continued to serve and protect the throne effectively for many years. Little else is written about 'the Three'. Sometimes being second best in the world's eyes is the best place to be.

Dearest Lord, when I am tempted to compare myself to others, free me to focus on what you've called me to do, and give me the energy to do it for your glory. Amen.

Genesis 16.1–13

Now Sarai, Abram's wife, had borne him no children. But she had an Egyptian servant named Hagar; so she said to Abram, 'The LORD has kept me from having children. Go, sleep with my servant; perhaps I can build a family through her.'

Abram agreed to what Sarai said. So after Abram had been living in Canaan ten years, Sarai his wife took her Egyptian servant Hagar and gave her to her husband to be his wife. He slept with Hagar, and she conceived. When she knew she was pregnant, she began to despise her mistress. Then Sarai said to Abram, 'You are responsible for the wrong I am suffering. I put my servant in your arms, and now that she knows she is pregnant, she despises me. May the LORD judge between you and me.'

'Your servant is in your hands,' Abram said. 'Do with her whatever you think best.' Then Sarai mistreated Hagar; so she fled from her.

The angel of the LORD found Hagar near a spring in the desert; it was the spring that is beside the road to Shur. And he said, 'Hagar, servant of Sarai, where have you come from, and where are you going?'

'I'm running away from my mistress Sarai,' she answered.

Then the angel of the LORD told her, 'Go back to your mistress and submit to her.' The angel added, 'I will increase your descendants so much that they will be too numerous to count.'

The angel of the LORD also said to her: 'You are now pregnant and you will give birth to a son. You shall name him Ishmael, for the LORD has heard of your misery. He will be a wild donkey of a man; his hand will be against everyone and everyone's hand against him, and he will live in hostility toward all his brothers.'

She gave this name to the LORD who spoke to her: 'You are the God who sees me,' for she said, 'I have now seen the One who sees me.'

Hagar: Strength in Difficult Relationships

Read the papers, watch certain television shows, and you gain a glimpse into hurting lives terribly damaged by complicated relationships. People are trying to salvage something in their turmoil. They sell their story with a cry of 'do you see my pain?' to a voyeuristic world.

Maybe Hagar, given the chance, would have sold her story too. After all, her barren mistress Sarai, with her wavering faith in God's promises, had given Hagar to her own husband Abram. Hagar becomes pregnant with the yearned-for son and heir, but this doesn't prove to be the easy solution Sarai has planned. Hagar now has little respect for her, and Sarai retaliates as her jealousy and bitterness erodes their relationship. Abram keeps his head down. After all, this isn't really his problem to deal with, he thinks.

The compulsion to run away is understandable and Hagar finds herself alone by a stream in the desert. The meaning of her name is 'stranger', and this has been the pattern for her lonely, servile existence. 'Does anyone see me?' is the cry of her heart.

In this desolate place, the angel of the Lord speaks into her life. He gives her new promises and tells her to return and submit to Sarai, possibly the last thing she'd want to do. In this transformational moment something powerful happens; Hagar knows that the depth of her pain has been seen. In her awareness of being deeply known and loved, Hagar is now able to respond to God's call.

Loving Lord, help me to remember that you know my troubles, and when you call me back into difficult situations, make me willing to follow. Amen.

1 Timothy 1.12–16

I thank Christ Jesus our Lord, who has given me strength, that he considered me faithful, appointing me to his service. Even though I was once a blasphemer and a persecutor and a violent man, I was shown mercy because I acted in ignorance and unbelief. The grace of our Lord was poured out on me abundantly, along with the faith and love that are in Christ Jesus.

Here is a trustworthy saying that deserves full acceptance: Christ Jesus came into the world to save sinners – of whom I am the worst. But for that very reason I was shown mercy so that in me, the worst of sinners, Christ Jesus might display his unlimited patience as an example for those who would believe on him and receive eternal life.

Paul: Transformed by Grace

St Paul saw himself as a supreme sinner. He had so rejected the grace of God that he persecuted Christians because they proclaimed Jesus, a man put to death on a cross, to be the Son of God. But on the road to Damascus, Paul had an unexpected encounter with the risen Christ and his life changed forever (Acts 9.1–19). From then on he became an apostle, following God's call to proclaim the good news of Jesus Christ to the Gentiles. Soon roles were reversed; *Paul* became the one who was persecuted and imprisoned for confessing the grace of God in Christ.

Today we could hail Paul as a hero, but I doubt that he would agree. Instead he would call himself the *worst* of sinners – he does it twice in this passage! If Paul, a sinner, is a hero of faith, it is not due to his own gifts and abilities; it is purely because of God's transforming grace in him. Paul is a prime example of God's ability to turn a life completely around.

We all have a past, things we've done of which we're not very proud. It's easy to convince ourselves that our failings disqualify us from serving God. Not so! Paul was able to view his past through the lens of God's grace and mercy, becoming an example through which Jesus' unlimited patience could be displayed. And if that's the case, then there's hope for us all.

Christ Jesus, you came into the world to save sinners. Thank you that there is nothing in my past or present which your grace and mercy cannot transform. Amen.

2 Kings 22.11–15, 19–23.3

When the king [Josiah] heard the words of the Book of the Law, he tore his robes. He gave these orders to Hilkiah the priest, Ahikam son of Shaphan, Akbor son of Micaiah, Shaphan the secretary and Asaiah the king's attendant: 'Go and inquire of the LORD for me and for the people and for all Judah about what is written in this book that has been found. Great is the LORD's anger that burns against us because those who have gone before us have not obeyed the words of this book; they have not acted in accordance with all that is written there concerning us.'

Hilkiah the priest, Ahikam, Akbor, Shaphan and Asaiah went to speak to the prophet Huldah, who was the wife of Shallum son of Tikvah, the son of Harhas, keeper of the wardrobe. She lived in Jerusalem, in the New Quarter. She said to them, 'This is what the LORD, the God of Israel, says: . . . "Because your heart was responsive and you humbled yourself before the LORD when you heard what I have spoken against this place and its people – that they would become a curse and be laid waste – and because you tore your robes and wept in my presence, I also have heard you, declares the LORD. Therefore I will gather you to your ancestors, and you will be buried in peace. Your eyes will not see all the disaster I am going to bring on this place."'

So they took her answer back to the king. Then the king called together all the elders of Judah and Jerusalem. He went up to the temple of the LORD with the people of Judah, the inhabitants of Jerusalem, the priests and the prophets – all the people from the least to the greatest. He read in their hearing all the words of the Book of the Covenant, which had been found in the temple of the LORD. The king stood by the pillar and renewed the covenant in the presence of the LORD – to follow the LORD and keep his commands, statutes and decrees with all his heart and all his soul, thus confirming the words of the covenant written in this book. Then all the people pledged themselves to the covenant.

Josiah: A Responsive Heart

Josiah is my favourite king in the Old Testament. It amazes me that he turned out so well, considering both his father and grandfather were terrible rulers!

When Josiah became king things improved significantly when he called for the repair of the temple. During the rebuilding the workers found something wonderful that had been neglected: the book of the law. When it was read to the king, Josiah humbled himself before the Lord and tore his clothes in repentance. This dramatic action expressed a responsive heart that was stirred to change by the words in the book of the law. Josiah changed the direction of his life and that of his nation.

As I read about Josiah's reaction I want to have a heart that is responsive like his. Josiah listened to his Lord's words, understood their implications, and responded decisively. Am I willing to do the same, even if it means costly change? God hears and blesses those who respond when they hear his word. Josiah's example shows us that the humble, responsive heart submits itself to the Lord. His action not only changed him, but also inspired many others to change their ways and follow God. Over the next thirteen years Josiah led a sweeping about-face, a reformation of Judah's faith, based on the law of God. Crucially, it all stemmed from the reformation God had brought about in his own, responsive heart.

Lord God, make my heart attentive to your word so like Josiah I may respond humbly in repentance and obedience. Amen.

John 11.17–36

On his arrival, Jesus found that Lazarus had already been in the tomb for four days. Now Bethany was less than two miles from Jerusalem, and many Jews had come to Martha and Mary to comfort them in the loss of their brother. When Martha heard that Jesus was coming, she went out to meet him, but Mary stayed at home.

'Lord,' Martha said to Jesus, 'if you had been here, my brother would not have died. But I know that even now God will give you whatever you ask.' Jesus said to her, 'Your brother will rise again.' Martha answered, 'I know he will rise again in the resurrection at the last day.' Jesus said to her, 'I am the resurrection and the life. Anyone who believes in me will live, even though they die; and whoever lives by believing in me will never die. Do you believe this?' 'Yes, Lord,' she told him, 'I believe that you are the Messiah, the Son of God, who was to come into the world.'

After she had said this, she went back and called her sister Mary aside. 'The Teacher is here,' she said, 'and is asking for you.' When Mary heard this, she got up quickly and went to him. Now Jesus had not yet entered the village, but was still at the place where Martha had met him. When the Jews who had been with Mary in the house, comforting her, noticed how quickly she got up and went out, they followed her, supposing she was going to the tomb to mourn there.

When Mary reached the place where Jesus was and saw him, she fell at his feet and said, 'Lord, if you had been here, my brother would not have died.'

When Jesus saw her weeping, and the Jews who had come along with her also weeping, he was deeply moved in spirit and troubled. 'Where have you laid him?' he asked. 'Come and see, Lord,' they replied. Jesus wept. Then the Jews said, 'See how he loved him!'

Mary: At Jesus' Feet

What do we do when it all goes wrong? What do we say to Jesus when our world is falling apart? When Jesus calls Mary to him following the death of her brother, the first thing she does is to fall at his feet. She comes before Jesus in her grief and pain and weeps. And he weeps with her.

This might remind us of two other occasions when Mary sat at Jesus' feet. The first is in Luke 10.38–42, when Jesus is at the home of Mary and Martha. Martha, the busy active one, is in the kitchen serving and preparing; but Mary, the quiet contemplative one, is sitting at Jesus' feet, listening to him. When Martha bemoans the fact that Mary is not helping her, Jesus says 'Mary has chosen what is better'. Mary knows the value of sitting with her Lord, listening to his words and making the most of his company.

Secondly, in John 12.1–8, we see Mary taking a bottle of expensive perfume, sitting at Jesus' feet and pouring the perfume over them, wiping them clean with her hair. Here we see Mary's humility before her Lord and her recognition of Jesus' worthiness as she anoints his feet. Mary worships Jesus in the high times, when all is well. Equally, she worships him in the low times, when all is far from well in her life.

How often do we, like Mary, find ourselves at the feet of our Lord? Mary discovered the value of doing so on several occasions: in recognition of his worthiness; to listen to his words; to lay her sorrows before him. She worshipped him.

Lord Jesus, teach me to be like Mary – at home at your feet, bringing my praise and sorrows, and learning from you. Amen.

John 9.8–11, 15–17, 24–28, 30

His neighbours and those who had formerly seen him begging asked, 'Isn't this the same man who used to sit and beg?' Some claimed that he was.

Others said, 'No, he only looks like him.'

But he himself insisted, 'I am the man.'

'How then were your eyes opened?' they asked.

He replied, 'The man they call Jesus made some mud and put it on my eyes. He told me to go to Siloam and wash. So I went and washed, and then I could see.'

Therefore the Pharisees also asked him how he had received his sight. 'He put mud on my eyes,' the man replied, 'and I washed, and now I see.'

Some of the Pharisees said, 'This man is not from God, for he does not keep the Sabbath.'

But others asked, 'How can a sinner perform such signs?' So they were divided.

Then they turned again to the blind man, 'What have you to say about him? It was your eyes he opened.'

The man replied, 'He is a prophet.'

A second time they summoned the man who had been blind. 'Give glory to God and tell the truth,' they said. 'We know this man is a sinner.'

He replied, 'Whether he is a sinner or not, I don't know. One thing I do know. I was blind but now I see!'

Then they asked him, 'What did he do to you? How did he open your eyes?'

He answered, 'I have told you already and you did not listen. Why do you want to hear it again? Do you want to become his disciples too?'

Then they hurled insults at him.

The man answered, 'Now that is remarkable! You don't know where he comes from, yet he opened my eyes.'

To this they replied, 'You were steeped in sin at birth; how dare you lecture us!' And they threw him out.

The Man Born Blind: Simple Testimony

John 9 is my favourite chapter in all of Scripture. It tells of a simple, honest man simply and honestly telling it as it is.

The religious leaders argue; they talk to the blind man twice; they question his parents and all the while this man sits in the middle of it all, enjoying his newfound sight and the beautiful world of colour and light that he is encountering for the first time. He is very matter-of-fact about what Jesus has done. In the end, this uneducated man who has never been able to read a single word of the law, ends up giving the Pharisees, the religious experts, a lesson in how to recognize a prophet. The one who was blind becomes the clearest thinking eye-witness. Brilliant!

The man born blind doesn't have any clever arguments and he doesn't give two hoots about theological sophistication. He simply says it as it is: 'I was blind but now I see'.

The strongest thing going for us when we try to share Christ with others is the reality of what God has done for us. If we have met Jesus, we have something concrete to share. What matters is not our eloquence, but the simple truth of Jesus' liberating power in our own lives.

We don't have to have all the answers. But, like the man born blind, in our own words we can honestly say 'I was blind but now I see'.

Lord Jesus, give me opportunities today to talk simply and honestly about you with the people around me. Amen.

Exodus 2.1–10

Now a man of the house of Levi married a Levite woman, and she became pregnant and gave birth to a son. When she saw that he was a fine child, she hid him for three months. But when she could hide him no longer, she got a papyrus basket for him and coated it with tar and pitch. Then she placed the child in it and put it among the reeds along the bank of the Nile. His sister stood at a distance to see what would happen to him.

Then Pharaoh's daughter went down to the Nile to bathe, and her attendants were walking along the riverbank. She saw the basket among the reeds and sent her female slave to get it. She opened it and saw the baby. He was crying, and she felt sorry for him. 'This is one of the Hebrew babies,' she said.

Then his sister asked Pharaoh's daughter, 'Shall I go and get one of the Hebrew women to nurse the baby for you?'

'Yes, go,' she answered. And the girl went and got the baby's mother. Pharaoh's daughter said to her, 'Take this baby and nurse him for me, and I will pay you.' So the woman took the baby and nursed him. When the child grew older, she took him to Pharaoh's daughter and he became her son. She named him Moses, saying, 'I drew him out of the water.'

Exodus 15.19–21

When Pharaoh's horses, chariots and horsemen went into the sea, the LORD brought the waters of the sea back over them, but the Israelites walked through the sea on dry ground. Then Miriam the prophet, Aaron's sister, took a timbrel in her hand, and all the women followed her, with timbrels and dancing. Miriam sang to them:

'Sing to the LORD,
  for he is highly exalted.
Both horse and driver
  he has hurled into the sea.'

Miriam: Humble Leadership

Miriam has been my personal hero ever since, at the age of ten, I chose her name to add to my own at confirmation. My reasoning then was that the way Miriam watched over the baby Moses was an excellent example for a big sister. She is protective of her little brother, bravely addressing Pharaoh's daughter, and her quick thinking reunites mother and son for a little longer.

Miriam next appears leading the women in worship after crossing the Red Sea. She happily sings exactly the same words that Moses and the men have just sung. All the Israelite women follow Miriam rather than Moses, but sing the same words of praise. In her example, Miriam points them towards God, not towards her brother.

Miriam's role is rarely centre-stage, even though she is a prophet herself. Instead she is seen standing at a distance or taking her cue from Moses. She wasn't perfect, but she clearly had a leadership role amongst the people of Israel; yet it was leadership from within the people, rather than at the head of them.

God may call us to lead from the front. For most of us, he is more likely to ask us to serve in the middle – or at the back. But even there we can still play a vital role in God's purposes; even there we may be crucial to another's current or future leadership; even there we can still be instrumental in pointing people towards God and enabling them to praise him for what he has done. May we be always ready to see God's people built up regardless of the prominence of our own role.

Lord, show me what gifts you have given to me, and give me humility to put them to right use in your service. Amen.

Jonah 1.11–12

The sea was getting rougher and rougher. So they asked him, 'What should we do to you to make the sea calm down for us?' 'Pick me up and throw me into the sea,' he replied, 'and it will become calm. I know that it is my fault that this great storm has come upon you.'

Jonah 2.1–7, 9

From inside the fish Jonah prayed
     to the LORD his God. He said:
'In my distress I called to the LORD,
     and he answered me.
From deep in the realm of the dead I called
     for help, and you listened to my cry.
You hurled me into the deep,
     into the very heart of the seas,
     and the currents swirled about me;
all your waves and breakers
     swept over me.
I said, 'I have been banished
     from your sight;
yet I will look again
     toward your holy temple.'
The engulfing waters threatened me,
     the deep surrounded me;
     seaweed was wrapped around my head.
To the roots of the mountains I sank down;
     the earth beneath barred me in forever.
But you, LORD my God,
     brought my life up from the pit.
What I have vowed I will make good.
     I will say, 'Salvation comes from the LORD'.'
And the LORD commanded the fish, and it vomited Jonah onto dry land.

Jonah: Overcoming Avoidance

It's not easy to find something good in Jonah to emulate. He deliberately sets sail in a direction directly opposite to God's will, and he causes a storm as a result. Unlike the pagan sailors (the real heroes in the first chapter!), he sleeps and doesn't do anything to help the situation. When confronted at last by them, he finally manages to confess who he is and admits his flight. But unlike the sailors who seek to spare his life, he won't talk to God. He'd rather be thrown overboard to save the ship.

God doesn't *require* Jonah to take this drastic action; Jonah could repent and the sailors could row in God's direction. Instead Jonah would prefer to go into the sea (another act of avoiding God). Not until he is about to drown in the depths does he finally cry out to God. Rather than letting him drown, God throws him a lifeline in a most unlikely way. God has a purpose for him to be a channel of blessing to many others – even though in the story, Jonah doesn't want them to prosper!

Not following God's instructions is a choice that sometimes leads to detours and unnecessary storms that were never intended for us. Nevertheless, avoidance is a game I often fall into playing. The story of Jonah reminds me that if I face heavy weather in my life by deliberately turning away from God, he does not give up on me. If I genuinely want to try again, his grace is sufficient to bring me back to dry land. In the long run, his good purposes will not be thwarted by my reluctance.

Loving heavenly Father, turn any wilful avoidance in me into joyful obedience and life in all its fullness for others. Amen.

Habakkuk 2.1; 3.17–19

I will stand at my watch
  and station myself on the ramparts;
I will look to see what he will say to me,
  and what answer I am to give to this complaint.

Though the fig tree does not bud
  and there are no grapes on the vines,
though the olive crop fails
  and the fields produce no food,
though there are no sheep in the pen
  and no cattle in the stalls,
yet I will rejoice in the LORD,
  I will be joyful in God my Saviour.
The Sovereign LORD is my strength;
  he makes my feet like the feet of a deer,
he enables me to tread on the heights.

Habakkuk: Costly Steadfastness

As the book of Habakkuk opens, the prophet sees only too clearly his people broken by strife and contention, full of violence and injustice towards one another. He cries out to God in his distress, longing for a response. And what a response he gets! Things will get even worse; the disaster will become a total catastrophe and the whole people will be given up into the hands of the Babylonians.

How Habakkuk's heart must have sunk. But he will not give up pleading for mercy for his people, as he reflects on how deeply their disobedience must have disappointed God. He still relies on God. Habakkuk's Almighty God *will* come, *will* deliver. Meanwhile Habakkuk will stay with his people into the desolate-sounding future, listening for his faithful God's word, regardless of whether he likes or understands it. Though bewildered and hurting, he promises to wait quietly for God to respond to his costly faithfulness. When I'm tempted to try to domesticate or customize God, I remember Habakkuk and give thanks for his reliance on a big, big God!

Habakkuk is also a hero in another way for me: he prefigures our Lord Jesus Christ who out of love and obedience was also content to wait, even in the hands of evil men, and to face disgrace, death and the dark of the tomb for his Father.

Father, when I face situations of desolation or pain, help me to cling to Habbakuk's vision of that day when the knowledge of your glory will fill the earth. In the name of your faithful one, Amen.

Mark 14.3-9

While he was in Bethany, reclining at the table in the home of Simon the Leper, a woman came with an alabaster jar of very expensive perfume, made of pure nard. She broke the jar and poured the perfume on his head. Some of those present were saying indignantly to one another, 'Why this waste of perfume? It could have been sold for more than a year's wages and the money given to the poor.' And they rebuked her harshly. 'Leave her alone' said Jesus. 'Why are you bothering her? She has done a beautiful thing to me. The poor you will always have with you, and you can help them any time you want. But you will not always have me. She did what she could. She poured perfume on my body beforehand to prepare for my burial. Truly I tell you, wherever the gospel is preached throughout the world, what she has done will also be told, in memory of her.'

The Woman Who Anointed Jesus: Reckless Love

With a pounding heart and sweaty palms, you walk in. At first they don't see you. You look at what you hold in your hands – everything that was dear to you, and all that you have. A voice in your head cries out, 'Don't be stupid, there's another way! He wouldn't want you to be reckless!' Another voice sneers and calls you a fool. You hold your breath; you feel every eye stripping you naked. Gently, you pour out all you have onto him. What will he do? What will he say? Gradually, your eyes dare to look at his. And suddenly you know what it is to love with reckless abandon. You had seen it in him before.

We don't even know her name, but we know that Jesus thought her beautiful, tender action of extreme generosity should be proclaimed alongside his defeat of death and his resurrection. An amazingly privileged place. This woman shows us a glimpse of extravagant grace: love with reckless abandon.

Reckless love is about giving up everything and risking being called a fool. It is about not letting weeds grow between our dreams, about clinging onto hope without calculating the risk. Reckless love is daring to love again after being rejected or losing someone close. It is about giving sacrificially despite clouds of doubt and confusion. Reckless love has no conditions, criteria, or regrets. It is not about weighing the costs against the benefits. Reckless love is about being human again. It is loving like we have never loved before.

Lord, help me to love you wholeheartedly, and to show the reckless extravagance of your grace towards the stranger, the unwanted, the unloved and the abandoned, as well as towards the friend. Amen.

Matthew 16.13–19

When Jesus came to the region of Caesarea Philippi, he asked his disciples, 'Who do people say the Son of Man is?'

They replied, 'Some say John the Baptist; others say Elijah; and still others, Jeremiah or one of the prophets.'

'But what about you?' he asked. 'Who do you say I am?'

Simon Peter answered, 'You are the Messiah, the Son of the living God.'

Jesus replied, 'Blessed are you, Simon son of Jonah, for this was not revealed to you by flesh and blood, but by my Father in heaven. And I tell you that you are Peter, and on this rock I will build my church, and the gates of death will not overcome it. I will give you the keys of the kingdom of heaven; whatever you bind on earth will be bound in heaven, and whatever you loose on earth will be loosed in heaven.'

Simon Peter: Eagerness

For years I really didn't get on with Peter. I thought he was an insensitive and boorish coward, a talkative show-off who asked inane questions. He never seemed to think things through before he spoke or acted, he just jumped in feet-first. I couldn't understand why Jesus rated him so highly. How could Peter be the rock on which the church would be built?

I realized eventually that the reason I didn't like Peter was because he exhibited those traits I like least in myself. Luckily, Jesus' love for me is as unconditional and as transforming as his love for Peter.

And, over time, I realized something else. Peter's weaknesses are actually symptoms of his most endearing characteristic: eagerness. It's an eagerness born out of love: an eagerness to get closer; to know more; to be caught up in the joy of Jesus' journey.

What I thought was showing off (Matthew 14.27–31) came from such eagerness to be with Jesus that he stepped out of the boat. His ill-considered offer to build shelters at the transfiguration (Matthew 17.1–5) came from a profound response to a revelation of God's glory. His rash act in Gethsemane (John 18.9–11) came from keen desire to protect Jesus.

In his eagerness he made many mistakes and learned many difficult lessons, often being rebuked by Jesus. But with each mistake he was strengthened for a ministry that was to unfold over three decades. And so I look to Peter for inspiration in my own often clumsy eagerness.

Lord God, thank you for your unconditional and transforming love. Bless me with Peter-like eagerness to come closer to you, and transform my clumsy responses into effective servanthood. Amen.

Luke 23.32–43

Two other men, both criminals, were also led out with him to be executed. When they came to the place called the Skull, they crucified him there, along with the criminals – one on his right, the other on his left. Jesus said, 'Father, forgive them, for they do not know what they are doing.' And they divided up his clothes by casting lots.

The people stood watching, and the rulers even sneered at him. They said, 'He saved others; let him save himself if he is God's Messiah, the Chosen One.'

The soldiers also came up and mocked him. They offered him wine vinegar and said, 'If you are the king of the Jews, save yourself.'

There was a written notice above him, which read: THIS IS THE KING OF THE JEWS.

One of the criminals who hung there hurled insults at him: 'Aren't you the Messiah? Save yourself and us!'

But the other criminal rebuked him. 'Don't you fear God,' he said, 'since you are under the same sentence? We are punished justly, for we are getting what our deeds deserve. But this man has done nothing wrong.'

Then he said, 'Jesus, remember me when you come into your kingdom.'

Jesus answered him, 'Truly I tell you, today you will be with me in paradise.'

The Thief on the Cross: Outrageous Hope

I have always disliked my Christian name. I am named after my father and at home was known as 'little . . .', even as an adult. It is a name popular with an older generation. Associations with a children's programme and the title of a satirical film have made for no end of teasing. I have always disliked my name.

The criminal lifts his head that was bowed down in pain, shame and despair. He sees the soldiers, the executioners, mocking this man Jesus crucified next to him, and gambling for a share of his possessions. He sees the religious leaders scoffing at the so-called King of the Jews. And then, the criminal on the far side joins the abuse; but this is too much. The criminal knows his guilt, but this Jesus, what has he done? And has he not just asked God to forgive them? Could this forgiveness also be for him? It was a hope, an outrageous hope, but he had to ask, in words that will be forever remembered.

'Jesus, remember me when you come into your kingdom.'

After my father died, I wondered aloud to God many times, 'did my father believe?' Some time later, a friend was talking to an evangelist and hospital chaplain and mentioned my name. The evangelist recognized the name and told the story of a man who had given his life to Jesus – my father. The thief on the cross offers us outrageous hope to the last, for ourselves and for those whom we love.

Jesus, from the example of the thief on the cross grant me hope, outrageous hope, for myself and for those for whom I pray. Amen.

John 19.38–42

Later, Joseph of Arimathea asked Pilate for the body of Jesus.
Now Joseph was a disciple of Jesus, but secretly because he
feared the Jews. With Pilate's permission, he came and took the
body away. He was accompanied by Nicodemus, the man who
earlier had visited Jesus at night. Nicodemus brought a mixture
of myrrh and aloes, about seventy-five pounds. Taking Jesus'
body, the two of them wrapped it, with the spices, in strips of
linen. This was in accordance with Jewish burial customs. At
the place where Jesus was crucified, there was a garden, and
in the garden a new tomb, in which no one had ever been laid.
Because it was the Jewish day of Preparation and since the
tomb was nearby, they laid Jesus there.

Nicodemus: Growing Faith

It is wonderful that Nicodemus who had first come to Christ by night (John 3), hiding from the glare of public recognition, became one of the men who buried Jesus.

In their first encounter, Nicodemus had begun his covert conversation by affirming that Jesus was from God, but he didn't understand much more than that. We see bravery in chapter seven when he tried to counsel caution to the chief priests and Pharisees in exercising judgement on Christ. Nicodemus' growing trust in Jesus was shouted down by his peers on the ruling council . . . though not by all; Joseph of Arimathea was also a member. These two devout men recognized something profoundly different in the strange, itinerant preacher from Galilee.

After the crucifixion the growing confidence of these men finally emerges. Boldly asking for Jesus' body, their faith came into the light on this the darkest day of all. In one sense Nicodemus did nothing out of the ordinary – wrapping the cold corpse in accordance with custom. But the quantity of burial treatments was extraordinary! This was generous, wonderful devotion. Perhaps it was intended to provide a burial fit for a king, for the King.

Nicodemus offers hope to those of us who are keenly aware of the limits of our faith. It's never too late to bring our faith in Jesus into the light. Great faith and public commitment has its beginnings in small steps of searching, and in taking risks for God.

Heavenly Father, help me to grow in faith, and to dare to bring that faith into public view so that others may meet you. Amen.

Philippians 2.5–11

In your relationships with one another, have the same attitude of mind Christ Jesus had:
  Who, being in very nature God,
    did not consider equality with God
  something to be used to his own advantage;
    rather, he made himself nothing
    by taking the very nature of a servant,
    being made in human likeness.
  And being found in appearance as a human being,
    he humbled himself
    by becoming obedient to death –
    even death on a cross!
  Therefore God exalted him to the highest place
    and gave him the name that is above every name,
  that at the name of Jesus every knee should bow,
    in heaven and on earth and under the earth,
    and every tongue acknowledge that Jesus Christ is Lord,
    to the glory of God the Father.

Hebrews 12.3

Consider him who endured such opposition from sinners, so that you will not grow weary and lose heart.

Revelation 14.12

This calls for patient endurance on the part of the people of God who keep his commands and remain faithful to Jesus.

2 Thessalonians 3.5

May the Lord direct your hearts into God's love and Christ's perseverance.

Jesus of Nazareth: Perseverance

It's difficult to pick out just one characteristic of Jesus. *Love* is obvious, but what's striking is how Christ manifests it. The author of Hebrews speaks of his faithfulness, prayerfulness, and obedience. Paul accents Jesus' self-giving in our passage from Philippians, but in the short phrase 'obedient *to* death' (literally '*until* death' or '*to the point of* death') he sums up a characteristic of Christ that made all the difference – his perseverance.

Although our Lord was tempted by the devil, perplexed by his followers' lack of faith, rejected by his own people, mocked and scourged by the Romans and ultimately crucified, he did not give up. We owe our lasting hope to his steadfast endurance.

Jesus calls his followers to a similar perseverance, enabled by the Holy Spirit. *Twice* in Matthew's gospel he said 'the one who endures to the end will be saved' (10.22; 24.13). The early church found in his example the inspiration for encouraging one another to stay faithful and to endure the way of suffering that would come with following Jesus.

Today, 'perseverance' is a word rarely heard; more common is 'endurance', but even that seems confined to sporting events that don't last very long. To be a Christian is to be in it for the long haul. The good news is that we aren't called to persevere on our own. The same power of God's Spirit that indwelt Jesus and raised him from the dead is at work in us, enabling us as we walk in his path.

Heavenly Father, thank you for your Son's endurance – even to death on a cross – and for the hope he gives. Grant me grace to persevere in a life of trust in you. Amen.

The Contributors

Jeremy Begbie
Chris Bessant
Gita Bond
Rich Burley
Mel Burley
Andy Byfield
Martin Castle
Jill Chatfield
Adrian Chatfield
Matt Coles
Graham Collingridge
Toby Crowe
Emma Crowe
Peter Edwards
Lydia Gaston
David Green
Mark Harris
Jeremy Haswell
Annette Hawkins
Richard Higginson
James Hill
Tina Hodgett
Ali Hogger
Jamie McKay
Philip Jenson

Emma Johnson
Jane Keiller
Richard Kew
Sam Leach
Nicky-Sue Leonard
David Lewis
Rachel Livesey
Catherine McBride
Charlie Moloney
Janice Moore
Chris Newman
Jeremy Parsons
Katherine Picot
Julia Powley
Marcus Purnell
Tiffer Robinson
Amy Robinson
Edward Scrase-Field
Jez Safford
Brian Streeter
Michael Thompson
Ali Walton
Tim Yau
Jane Yeadon

At Ridley Hall we teach and practice sacrificial giving. Although most of the proceeds from the sale of this book will go to the College's development fund, ten percent will be given away, together with money saved from weekly frugal lunches and other activities. As part of our commitment to mission, the students here decide each year corporately to support three different mission partners. This year the partners we are supporting are:

Bob & Jane Hurley in Tanzania: Bob teaches at the Bible College near Morogoro, training pastors and joining them in evangelism and church planting. Jane works with young women and mothers. For more information visit:
http://web.mac.com/bobhurley

Alexandria School of Theology: Founded in 2005 by Bishop Mouneer Anis (now the Anglican Primate of the Middle East), this institution aims to equip indigenous Christians to reach the Middle East for Christ. For more information visit:
http://www.ast-eg.org

Bill & Irene Manley in Mongolia: Bill and Irene have set up 'Mary & Martha Mongolia', an attempt to do 'business as mission'. For more information visit:
http://www.mmmongolia.com

About Ridley Hall

When Ridley Hall first opened its doors in Cambridge in the 1880s, even the wildest optimist could not have predicted the impact it would have for Jesus Christ in the UK and around the world. Today the College not only forms men and women for ordination in the Church of England and in the greater Anglican Communion, but also trains youth leaders, and undertakes a host of other activities to equip lay Christians for their ministries in a rapidly changing world.

To find out more about Ridley and all that we do, please visit our website:

www.ridley.cam.ac.uk

If you have appreciated the devotions in this book and would like to be more involved in the life of Ridley Hall, please get in touch with us. There is much here that may be of help to you in your own Christian discipleship, as you will see from our website.

Raising up 21st century leaders to tackle the unique challenges of today requires courage, creativity, and significant resources. We invite you to:

- Pray for Ridley's ministry
- Become a regular donor to our work
- Make a gift of stocks or shares to Ridley Hall
- Include Ridley in your estate planning
- Encourage others to become part of the wider Ridley community

For more information, please contact Ridley Hall's Development Office (development@ridley.cam.ac.uk or call us on 01223 741079).

Ridley Hall is a registered charity (no. 311456) and is a member of the Cambridge Theological Federation.

Index of Bible Passages Cited